Reader's Workout

PRACTICE BOOK

Program Author

David W. Moore

Text Credits
Page 125 "As Obesity Rates Rise, Schools Reconsider Vending-Machine Contracts" by Camille Ricketts © McClatchy Tribune Information Services. All Rights Reserved. Reprinted with permission.

PHOTOGRAPHS:
Alamy Limited: p153 (Julian Beever © Justin Kase/Alamy).
AP Images: p199 (Dolores Huerta © Rich Pedroncelli).
Artville: p45 (salad).
Becky Thurman: p140 (signing) Photo 2006 by Becky Thurman, Georgia Perimeter College (www.gpc.edu/~gpcslip).
Bobby Hansson: p146 (playing tin horn) Courtesy of Bobby Hansson.
Bruce Coleman Inc.: p26 (Diana monkey © Mark Newman); p32 (deforestation © Wolfgang Bayer).
CORBIS: p2 (Beijing-Lhasa train © Wu Hong/epa); p5 ('L' train in Chicago © Randy Faris); p13 (cloud forest on mountains © Michael & Patricia Fogden); p19 (terra cotta warriors © Kristi J. Black); p35 (John Muir © CORBIS): p36 (Muir Glacier © Tom Bean); p37 (NASCAR Race © George Tiedemann/NewSport); p40 (Erik Weihenmayer © Didrik Johnck); p41 (Amelia Earhart © Bettmann); p48 (Bethany after accident © Kirk Aeder/Icon SMI); p61 (ski patrol with dog © Thinkstock); p63 (skyscraper worker © CORBIS); p65 (tornado chaser © Jim Reed); p66 (commercial diver © Bettmann); p67 (surfer at Mavericks © Frederic Larson/San Francisco Chronicle); p75 (Matthew Henson © Bettmann); p82 (climber sleeping © Aaron Black/Solus-Veer); p84 (top of El Capitan © David Muench); p110 ("Master Mystifier" poster © Bettmann); p117 (John Hancock Center © Hisham Ibrahim); p145 (license plate © Andrew Lichtenstein); p170 (patrol at night © Kristi J. Black); p172 (empty downtown street © Brendan Regan); p175 (milkshake on counter © ROB & SAS); p178 (rafflesia 22 © Frans Lanting); p182 (high school girl and boy © Jon Feingers/zefa); p195 Jane Addams © Underwood & Underwood); p196 (Arthur Ashe © Hulton-Deutsch Collection).
Danita Delimont Stock Photography: p64 (bush plane © John Warburton-Lee).
David Barzelay: p169 (curfew sign) Courtesy of David Barzelay.
Everett Collection, Inc.: p95 (Star Trek ship © UPN / Courtesy: Everett Collection); p157 (1937 workers on strike Courtesy: CSU Archives/Everett Collection).
Fotosearch.com: p3 (teen driver with eyes closed © Digital Vision); p11 studious male teen © Digital Vision); p139 left (ASL sign "help" © LushPix); p139 upper right (ASL signs "hope" © LushPix); p139 lower right (ASL sign "I love you" © LushPix).
Getty Images: p6 (students in science class © Frank Herrmann/Taxi); p7 (young guitarist © Gustavo Di Mario); p28 (teen boy © Paul Taylor); p38 (checkered flag © David Madison/Photographer's Choice); p43 (Zadie Smith © David Levenson); p44 (S.E. Hinton © Ed Lallo/Time & Life Pictures); p51 (Dr. Kernard Kouchner © DOMINIQUE FAGET/AFP); p52 (surgery © Per-Amders Pettersson); p68 (Grant Twiggy Baker © Pierre Tostee/ASP); p73 (woman snorkeling © Charles Gullung/Photonica); p76 (Henson @ North Pole w/ other explorers © Robert Peary/Hulton Archive); p92 (meteorite crater © J R EVERMAN/Time & Life Pictures); p93 (holding large carrot © Noel Hendrickson/Digital Vision); p105 (Humboldt squid © BRIAN J SKERRY/National Geographic); p126 (cafeteria © Yellow Dog Productions); p154 (chalk © Steve Weinrebe); p158 (children huddling ©Jacob A. Riis); p159 (microchip size comparison © Jeff Sherman); p171 (cell phone screen © Stuart Gregory); p177 (tropical pitcher plant © Joseph Van Os/The Image Bank); p179 (skier in a slalom race © Zoom Agence); p185 (homeless woman © PhotoAlto Agency); p187 (destruction from tsunami of Dec. 24, 2004 © Paula Bronstein).
Index Stock Imagery: p83 (female climber © Greg Epperson).
Jupiter Images: p42 (stunt plane © Walter Giordani/Workbook Stock); p74 (diving equipment © Image Source); p74 (headlamp © Hemera Technologies); p121 (empty stage with microphone © Verity Smith/Brand X Pictures); p191 (female working out © Corbis).
Library of Congress: p109 (Houdini's milk can trick).
March of Dimes Birth Defects Foundation: p50 (newspapers) Courtesy of March of Dimes Birth Defects Foundation.
National Geographic Image Collection: p25 (prairie dog © MICHAEL MELFORD): p81 (El Capitan © MARC MORITSCH).
Noah Hamilton Photography: p47 (Bethany Hamilton © Noah Hamilton Photography).
Ohio State Historical Society: p59 (suffragists) Courtesy of the Ohio State Historical Society.
Peter Arnold, Inc.: p14 (brown howler monkey © Luiz C. Marigo); p24 (hurricane © Weatherstock).
PhotoEdit, Inc.: p87 (blind person w/ cane © David Young-Wolff); p111 (Polar Bear Plunge © Lon C. Diehl); p137 (two teens using sign language © Myrleen Ferguson Cate); p138 (child with a cochlear implant © Michael Newman); p190 (police searching apartment © Rhoda Sidney); p192 (students running track © Park Street).
PhotoLibrary: p193 (Inuits hunting © Yvette Cardozo Card).
Reuters: p156 (Julian Beever © Kevin Lamarque/Reuters).
Robert Manduchi: p88 (virtual cane) Courtesy of Robert Manduchi.
SuperStock, Inc.: p183 (teenaged girl using a video camera © Pixtal).
The Granger Collection, New York: p49 (Jonas Salk); p57 (Victoria Woodhull).
The Image Works: p60 (Victoria Woodhull turned away © Mary Evans Picture Library); p112 (Polar Bear Plunge festival © Sean Cayton); p121 (performing on stage © Bob Daemmrich).
The National Archives: p132 (Virginia Hall) Joint Chiefs of Staff, Office of Strategic Services.

ILLUSTRATIONS:
Dartmouth Publishing, Inc.: All illustrations except p39. **Emil Huston:** p39.

National Geographic School Publishing
Hampton-Brown
P.O. Box 223220
Carmel, California 93922
800-333-3510
www.NGSP.com

Printed in the United States of America

Practice Book TAE
978-0-7362-3487-0

Practice Book
978-0-7362-3486-3

07 08 09 10 11 12 13 14 15 9 8 7 6 5 4 3 2 1

Contents

Unlocking Words

Your Job as a Reader

Active Reading

Strategy 1: Plan and Monitor Your Reading

Strategy 6: Make Inferences

Strategy 7: Synthesize

Strategy Wrap-Up: Putting It All Together

Comprehension Skills in Action

Name ____________________ Date __________

Word Families

Read "Opening an Isolated Land." Use word families to predict the meaning of each underlined word. Write your prediction on the self-stick note.

Strategy at a Glance

Word Families

A **word family** is a group of words that look alike and are related in meaning.

When you come across a new word, look closely to see if it reminds you of another word.

DID YOU KNOW?

- China governs the independent region of Tibet.
- A train ride from Beijing, China, to Lhasa, Tibet, takes 48 hours.

OPENING AN ISOLATED LAND

For generations, Tibet has been isolated due to its rugged landscape. Dangerous elevations and unreliable roads made traveling very difficult. Located at the top of a **lofty plateau**, Tibet saw few visitors. Now, a modern railway has penetrated its forbidding **terrain**.

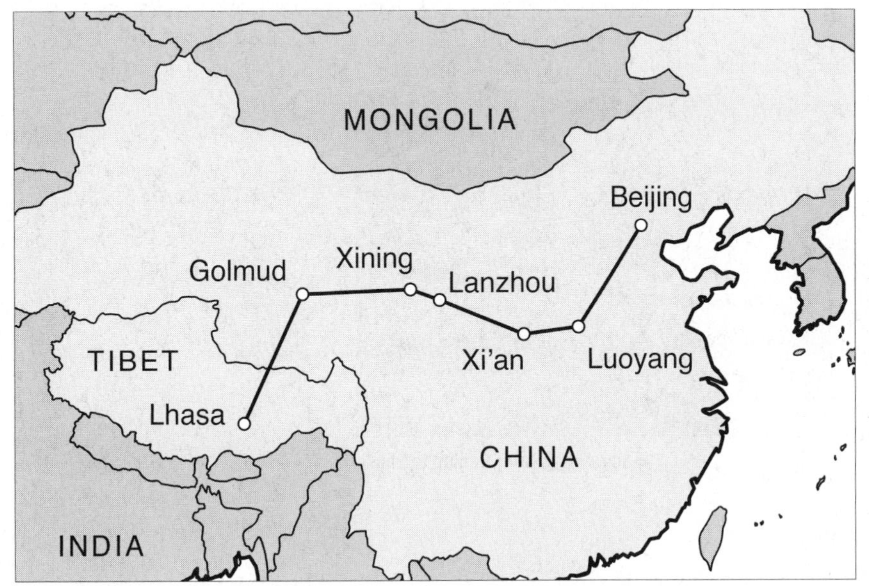

Route from Beijing, China, to Lhasa, Tibet

The majority of the rail track is thousands of feet above sea level. At this height, the air contains about half as much oxygen as it does at sea level. Breathing this thin air is exhausting and dangerous, so construction workers worked only six hours daily.

continued on next page

lofty *adj.*, high
plateau *n.*, flat top of a hill or mountain range
terrain *n.*, type of land

1. isolated
   - related words:
   - I think it means:

2. elevations
   - related words:
   - I think it means:

3. unreliable
   - related words:
   - I think it means:

4. construction
   - related words:
   - I think it means:

Opening an Isolated Land, continued

The climate was also a fierce opponent. Drastic changes in temperature would destroy building materials. Workers pumped **coolants** into the ground to keep it frozen. Frozen ground supported the tracks and kept the building materials **intact**. The natural landscape was an additional challenge. The mountains were higher and the rivers were wider than engineers had ever experienced. Yet, they found technological solutions and built track up and across these obstacles.

The project to link Beijing to Lhasa by rail was a success. Passengers can ride from the busy urban streets of the Chinese capital to the rugged and beautiful wilds of Tibet. Within the safety of the pressurized cabin, only the beautiful views of the mountains take their breath away. Once it was nearly impossible to travel to Tibet. Now many people can arrive in style.

The railroad from Beijing to Lhasa

coolants *n.*, substances that cool things
intact *adj.*, undamaged, complete

5. opponent
   - related words:
   - I think it means:

6. additional
   - related words:
   - I think it means:

7. pressurized
   - related words:
   - I think it means:

Talk About It

Tell a classmate how you used word families.

Make the Ideas Your Own

What did you learn about Tibet from the selection?

Name ________________________ Date __________

Context Clues

As you read "Smart, Safe Cars," circle the clues to the meaning of each underlined word. Use the clues to predict its meaning. Write your prediction on the self-stick note.

Look for these kinds of clues:
- a direct definition, often signaled by *is, called, refers to,* or *means*
- a restatement, set off by commas and often beginning with *or*
- a synonym, often signaled by *also* or *like*
- an antonym, often signaled by *but* or *unlike*
- examples, often signaled by *such as, for example,* or *including*

Strategy at a Glance

Context Clues

When you read and come across a new word, look for clues in the surrounding words.

DID YOU KNOW?
- Sleepy drivers are responsible for more than 100,000 car accidents each year.
- Drowsy driving is illegal in New Jersey.

Smart, Safe Cars

Suppose you went to bed at 12 A.M. Now it's 2 in the afternoon. Your head is nodding. The muscles in your face slacken, or relax. You can barely stay awake in class. "Tyler! Snap out of it," barks the teacher. Outside of a little embarrassment, you're fine. Yet, if you had been driving, you might have been in serious danger.

Nodding off behind the wheel can be deadly.

Automakers are turning to new technology to prevent tragedies. Car manufacturers have discovered that the human face is part of the solution. They are working with researchers to develop a camera that will **monitor** the facial expressions of drivers. The specialized camera communicates with a computer program in the car. Then the system gets smart. It monitors the movements of the driver's lips and eyelids. When the driver's facial movements **indicate** drowsiness, the steering wheel vibrates. The car wakes the driver.

continued on next page

monitor *v.*, keep track of
indicate *v.*, show

1. I think slacken means:

2. I think automakers means:

3. I think facial expressions means:

Smart, Safe Cars, continued

Tests have shown that this technology is effective. They have encouraged automakers to develop more safety innovations, such as a crash control computer that will actually prevent crashes. First, the smart windshield has a sensor that takes in the speed and distance of other cars. It passes this information to an onboard computer that calculates when a crash is likely. A smart car with this device slams on the brakes even if the driver does not.

Today's engineers develop solutions using algorithms. Algorithms are procedures for solving problems. Scientists use these procedures to create reliable and **accurate** safety systems. These systems recognize human needs and human mistakes. Someday, smarter cars may prevent mistakes from becoming disasters.

accurate *adj.*, exact, without errors

4. I think innovations means:

5. I think algorithms means:

Now complete the chart and compare your predictions to the definitions in a dictionary.

Underlined Word	Kind of Clue	What Meaning Did You Predict?	What Is the Dictionary Definition?
1. slacken			
2. automakers			
3. facial expressions			
4. innovations			
5. algorithms			

Talk About It

Compare the meanings you predicted with a partner's.

Make the Ideas Your Own

What do you want to remember about smart cars?

Name ______________________ Date __________

Multiple-Meaning Words

Study the dictionary entries. Each entry word is a multiple-meaning word—it has more than one definition.

Strategy at a Glance

Use Context Clues

When you read a word that has more than one meaning, use clues in the surrounding words to figure out which meaning makes the most sense.

fly *n.* an insect with transparent wings *v.* **1** : to use wings to move through the air **2** : to move quickly

point *n.* **1** : a sharp end **2** : a particular time **3** : the main idea *v.* to aim

track *n.* **1** : evidence that a person or vehicle leaves behind such as footprints **2** : rails of a railroad **3** : grooves on a record or tape *v.* to follow or search for something

These multiple-meaning words are underlined in "Slow Motion." As you read, circle the clues to the meaning of each underlined word. Write the correct meaning on the self-stick note.

DID YOU KNOW?

- Chicago Transit Authority is the second largest public transportation system in the U.S.

Slow Motion

Chicago's elevated train

Residents of big cities take buses and trains for granted. In Chicago, the public transportation system serves half a million citizens daily. In 2007, Chicago Transit Authority (CTA) began the process of **renovating** a portion of its elevated train tracks. The point of the project was to help commuters. Workers would increase the size of platforms to **accommodate** longer trains. New elevators would make the stations accessible for passengers with disabilities.

The project resulted in some **predictable** but temporary side effects. Some trains that used to fly along the track slowed to a crawl. Passengers' routines were disrupted. A half-hour ride home stretched to an hour. Despite occasional problems, people still want the convenience of public transportation. The number of passengers is now at its highest level in five decades.

renovating *v.*, fixing up
accommodate *v.*, to make room for
predictable *adj.*, could be expected beforehand

1. Here, the word tracks means:

2. Here, the word point means:

3. Here, the word fly means:

As you read "Insect Clues," circle the clues to the meaning of *fly* and *point*. Then write the correct meaning on the self-stick note.

DID YOU KNOW?

- Many popular television shows are about solving crimes.
- Forensics uses science to help solve crimes.

Insect Clues

Students work in a lab to solve a science mystery.

The class "Crime Solving Insects" is a little bit like a popular TV show. But these student **sleuths** use insects to figure out why an animal died. First, they learn that a type of fly feeds on dead animals. Wasps arrive later to feed on these infant flies, or maggots. Students study insect life cycles. They examine models that look like maggots. Then, the teachers present the **novice** detectives with different **scenarios**. Each scenario includes an animal death. The teacher challenges the students to explain each scenario. At this point, students have enough new knowledge to solve the mysteries.

---

sleuths *n.*, detectives
novice *adj.*, newly-skilled
scenarios *n.*, situations

4. Here, the word fly means:

5. Here, the word point means:

Talk About It

With a partner, talk about other words in the passages that have multiple meanings.

Make the Ideas Your Own

What did you learn about public transportation from the first selection?

____

____

What did you learn about insects from the second selection?

____

____

Name ______________________ Date ____________

Jargon

As you read "Five Minutes with Heavy Weather," circle the clues to the meaning of each underlined word. Use the clues to predict its meaning. Write your prediction on a self-stick note.

Strategy at a Glance

Use Context Clues

Jargon is the specialized and technical vocabulary used by a particular group of people.

When you come across jargon, look for clues in the surrounding words to figure it out.

Five Minutes with Heavy Weather

CD Magazine interviewed Julio Garza of Heavy Weather.

Julio Garza, lead guitarist of Heavy Weather

CD: Your band is known for mixing its sounds. Describe the music you make.

JG: That's a tough one. We like to **fuse** different genres. We tend to feed on the **improv** spirit of jazz, especially during our live shows. But our base is definitely hard-rocking indie music.

CD: How do you start writing a piece of music?

JG: Well, we usually begin with a hip-hop beat or a guitar riff and sort of go from there. Once we have a solid hook, though, we can fly.

CD: What's next for Heavy Weather?

JG: We have a new album that includes some old-school reggae music. Man, we're loving those rhythms right now.

Look for Heavy Weather's new CD this summer.

---

fuse *v.*, combine
improv *adj.*, abbreviation for *improvisation*

1. I think genres means:

2. I think riff means:

3. I think hook means:

Use a resource to confirm your predictions.

Jargon	What Meaning Did You Predict?	How Did You Confirm the Meaning?
1. genres		Resource:
2. riff		Resource:
3. hook		Resource:

Continue to circle the context clues to figure out the jargon in "Communication Masters." Write the predicted meaning on the self-stick note.

DID YOU KNOW?

- In 2004, 75% of teens sent instant messages.
- *Webspeak* is the slang and abbreviated terms teens use to text, blog, and IM.

Communication Masters

When my parents were my age, the landline telephone was the center of their universe. I hardly ever use a regular phone to make calls. Why would I, when I could reach a friend more quickly with pictures, even movies, using my cell or my laptop?

Yesterday was the perfect example. I was sitting on the couch, bored. "WU?" I asked my friend Ana. Turns out, I wasn't the only one who was bored. Soon, every SMS device within a three-block **radius** was buzzing. A bunch of us agreed to meet at Ana's house to play music.

Later that afternoon, I went home to find the whole event written up in Tranh's blog. His post began with a picture of my guitar solo. Mom yelled that dinner was ready just as I was linking my own pix to Tranh. "G2G," I IM'd on my cell. "TTYL."

I just can't imagine how my parents ever managed to have a social life talking on a telephone.

radius *n.*, distance from a central point

4. I think WU means:

5. I think IM'd means:

Jargon	What Meaning Did You Predict?	How Did You Confirm the Meaning?
4. WU?		Resource:
5. IM'd		Resource:

Talk About It

Tell a classmate how you figured out the meanings of the underlined words. Compare the meanings you predicted.

Make the Ideas Your Own

What jargon do you use? Does everyone understand it? Explain.

Name ____________________ Date __________

Compound Words

As you read "The Trivia Tournament," circle the parts of each underlined compound word. Write the predicted meaning on the self-stick note.

Strategy at a Glance

Use Word Parts

A **compound word** is a word made up of two or more smaller words.

When you come across a long word, look to see if you know any of its parts.

DID YOU KNOW?

- Each year in Wisconsin, about 12,000 people compete in the world's largest trivia contest.
- The contest lasts for 54 hours without stopping.

The Trivia Tournament

"Have you heard about Cruz?" Eric burst into my room waving a newspaper. "Praiseworthy performance by Alexandra Cruz. She's won three major **trivia** contests. You'll compete against her next week." Eric hoped this news would put some fire in me, because I never studied, even though I was defending my Teen Trivia Champion title for the last time before I turned eighteen.

"Have a look," Eric said. "This girl is only 16."

I **skimmed** the article. "This is the easiest winning question I've ever heard!" I said with some **revulsion**. "Everyone knows the deepest freshwater lake is in Siberia."

Eric rolled his eyes. "You might be overconfident."

I shrugged. In my mind, I could handle anything the judges could ask me. I dripped facts. The Third Russian Revolution was a fight against the Bolsheviks. Beethoven wrote the *Moonlight Sonata* in 1801. I amazed everyone.

---

trivia *n.*, little known facts
skimmed *v.*, quickly read
revulsion *n.*, disgust

1. I think praiseworthy means:

2. I think freshwater means:

3. I think overconfident means:

Talk About It

Compare your predicted meanings to a partner's.

Make the Ideas Your Own

Do you know someone like the narrator of the story? How would you describe him or her?

____

____

____

Name ______________________ Date ____________

Prefixes

Study the prefixes and their meanings. As you read "Some Teens Have the Answers," circle the word parts in each underlined word. Use the parts to predict the meaning, and write it on the self-stick note.

Strategy at a Glance

Use Word Parts

A **prefix** is a word part added to the beginning of a word. It changes the word's meaning.

When you come across a new word, look to see if you know any of its parts.

Prefix	Meaning	Key Words
im-	not	imperfect, immature
re-	again	reelect, repay
over-	over	overreact, overpay

DID YOU KNOW?

- Low self-esteem and peer pressure are two common problems among teens.
- Solutions exist even for very unusual problems.

Some Teens Have the Answers

When you are in the middle of a **predicament**, it's often impossible to understand how you got there. You can learn how to adjust to problems as they arise, or you can learn management tools to prevent them from happening in the first place.

Do You Have Too Much to Do?

Before you have a mountain of things to do, ask yourself this question: *What's most important to me?* Reorganize your schedule so that you give **priority** to activities that help you meet your goals.

Many teens take on too much. When you feel overburdened by work and hobbies, you can't do your best. That's why it's better to focus on the things that are really most important to you.

predicament *n.,* problem
priority *n.,* more attention

1. I think impossible means:

2. I think reorganize means:

3. I think overburdened means:

Name ______________________ Date __________

Suffixes

Study the suffixes and their meanings. As you read the rest of the passage, circle the word parts in each underlined word. Use the parts to predict the meaning, and write it on the self-stick note.

Suffix	Meaning	Key Words
-ly	in a certain way	slowly, wisely
-ful	full of	joyful, hopeful
-ment	action or process of	payment, movement

Strategy at a Glance

Use Word Parts

A **suffix** is a word part that is added to the end of a word. It changes the word's meaning and its part of speech.

When you come across a new word, look to see if you know any of its parts.

Some Teens Have the Answers, continued

Do You Ever Wish You Could Rewrite Your Autobiography?

You can't rewrite your past. But happily, you can plan your future. Listen to suggestions from your family, teachers, and other people you trust. When they offer good advice, successful teens listen and consider if it **applies** to them.

Do Your Choices Reflect Who You Are?

Consider your **aspirations** for the future. You may know what the best choices are. Don't feel pressured by what your friends may say. Remember, the people who change the world are often the ones who use their own judgment.

continued on next page

Work toward your goals.

applies *v.*, fits
aspirations *n.*, hopes

1. I think happily means:

2. I think successful means:

3. I think judgment means:

Name ______________________ Date ____________

Prefixes and Suffixes

Study the prefixes and suffixes below. As you read the rest of the passage, continue to circle the word parts in each underlined word. Each word contains a prefix and a suffix. Use the word parts to predict the meaning, and write it on the self-stick note.

Strategy at a Glance

Use Word Parts

Prefixes and **suffixes** are word parts. They change the meaning of a base word.

When you come across a new word, look to see if you know any of its parts.

Prefix	Suffix	Meaning	Key Words
un-		not	unhappy, unclear
	-ly	in a certain way	slowly, probably
	-able	can be done	lovable, believable
pre-		before	prehistoric, preschool
	-ion	act or process of	celebration, action

Some Teens Have the Answers, continued

Do You Tap Into Your Community?

Unfortunately, some teens don't realize all the **resources** they have at hand. There are many people and places you can turn to for ideas, help, and information. The first place to look is at home. Which neighbors, family, and friends do you trust? You may discover that your uncle has had experiences that you can draw on. Or, your neighbor may know someone ready to offer you an unforgettable job.

Consider the resources in your town. Is there a **recreation** center or a counselor at your church, synagogue, or mosque? Set aside your preconceptions about asking for help. Take advantage of all the people and places that are in your community.

resources *n.*, sources of help and support
recreation *adj.*, having to do with relaxation and sports

1. I think unfortunately means:

2. I think preconceptions means:

Talk About It

Tell a classmate or your teacher how you used word parts to figure out the meanings of the words in the passage.

Make the Ideas Your Own

What did you learn about successful teens from the passage?

Name ______________________ Date ____________

Roots

Study the roots and their meanings below. As you read "Forests in the Clouds," circle the root in each underlined word. Use the word parts to predict the meaning, and write it on the self-stick note.

Strategy at a Glance

Use Word Parts

A **root** is a central word part that has meaning but cannot stand on its own.

When you come across a new word, look to see if you know any of its parts.

Root	Meaning	Key Words
cred	believe	credit, credential
struct	build	structure, construct
pop	people	popular, populate
bio	life	biography, biographical
scrib	write	scribble, transcription
fract, frag	break	fracture, fragment

DID YOU KNOW?

- There are cloud forests on many continents.
- Most cloud forests are found near the equator.

Forests in the Clouds

A cloud forest is an island in the sky. It is home to an incredible variety of plant and animal species. This rare type of rainforest found atop tropical mountains is in danger of destruction. If cloud forests disappear, the homes of many plants and animals will disappear with the clouds.

If you lived in a cloud forest, your home would often be covered in misty fog. The cooler air allows clouds to form.

Cloud forests are like natural water towers. They supply clean water to populations in cities and to industries.

continued on next page

A cloud forest in Cordillera de Tilaran, Costa Rica

1. I think incredible means:

2. I think destruction means:

3. I think populations means:

Continue to read the passage and circle the root in each underlined word. Write the predicted meaning on a self-stick note.

Forests in the Clouds, continued

Cloud forests provide more than water. More treasures are **shrouded** in the fog than anyone realizes. Percy Nuñez, a biologist in Peru, has discovered 30,000 to 40,000 plants. According to Nuñez, this is only the beginning. "So far, we have described only 20 percent of the species—plants and animals—that live in this almost vertical landscape," he says. The species Nuñez categorizes are mostly **endemic** to the area.

Cloud forests are delicate ecosystems. Deforestation, global warming, and pollution threaten them. However, replanting can help restore the fragile forest. And groups can focus the attention of the public on this natural treasure. For every day that the cloud forests are saved, a new natural treasure can be found.

Howler monkeys live in cloud forests.

shrouded *adj.,* hidden
endemic *adj.,* native

4. I think biologist means:

5. I think described means:

6. I think fragile means:

Talk About It

Tell a classmate or your teacher about other words you know with the roots *bio, cred,* and *struct.*

Make the Ideas Your Own

Why is preserving the cloud forests important?

Name ______________________ Date ____________

Denotation and Connotation

Read "The Mystery of Oak Island." Think about the connotation of each underlined word. Label each word to show its connotation—positive, negative, or neutral.

Strategy at a Glance

Go Beyond the Literal Meaning

The **denotation** of a word is its dictionary definition. The **connotation** is the feeling associated with it.

When you read, think about the meanings of the writer's words and how they make you feel.

DID YOU KNOW?

- Oak Island is located in Nova Scotia, Canada.

THE MYSTERY OF OAK ISLAND

Daniel was sixteen years old when he got the thirst for treasure. It all began in 1795. He and two friends had been wandering on Oak Island near their home. They saw an enormous **depression** in the earth. Joking about pirates' booty, they had gone for their shovels and began digging at the mysterious spot.

Clunk! After digging only two feet, they hit something. Daniel scraped off the stubborn dirt and saw several large **flagstones.** Eager to reach the treasure, the three boys removed the flagstones, and continued digging into the soft earth. Ten feet down, they struck the second clue. A layer of oak logs blocked the way, just as the flagstones had.

This did not deter the boys. They paused and looked intently at what lay beneath them. Finally, Daniel spoke up. His voice was steady.

treasure: positive

1. enormous:

2. stubborn:

3. Eager:

4. steady:

continued on next page

depression *n.*, dent

flagstones *n.*, flat paving stones

As you read the rest of the passage, label each underlined word to show its connotation.

The Mystery of Oak Island, continued

"Well, someone has taken great trouble to cover this hole. It must hold a treasure," Daniel said. Confident they would solve the mystery, the boys **persevered**. One day of digging grew into two, and then three. Finally, at thirty feet, Daniel stopped.

5.

"It's hopeless with only our shovels," he whined.

6.

The mystery hole captivated them, even as they grew into men. The three saved money, purchased heavy digging equipment, and set to work again. At ninety feet, they unearthed a stone. They wiped off the dirt and discovered a message, but no expert could interpret the strange language.

7.

8.

Eventually, interest in the project died for Daniel and his friends. Yet the hole on Oak Island and the **cryptic** message on the stone continued to spark curiosity in many, who continue to take up the search to this day.

9.

---

persevered *v.*, kept trying
captivated *v.*, fascinated
cryptic *adj.*, puzzling

Talk About It

Compare your connotation labels with a partner's. Discuss how each underlined word made you feel.

Make the Ideas Your Own

What does the story remind you of? Explain why.

Name ______________________ Date ____________

Idioms

As you read "Natural Lights," circle the clues to the meaning of each underlined idiom. Then write the predicted meaning on the self-stick note.

Strategy at a Glance

Go Beyond the Literal Meaning

In an **idiom**, the phrase as a whole means something different from what the words mean by themselves.

When you come across an idiom,

- look for clues to its meaning in the surrounding words
- make a guess that makes sense.

DID YOU KNOW?

- The Aurora Borealis, or Northern Lights, fills the night sky with colorful clouds and rays of light.
- It has been seen from Alaska to as far south as Mexico.

Natural Lights

Last fall, a new family moved in next door. They were from the city, and complained to everyone about our small town. "I have to be here in the sticks, but I don't have to like it," Joe sneered. I felt sorry for the newcomer, but he seemed to have a big chip on his shoulder.

I decided to show Joe one of the **advantages** of living here. My buddy Manuel, a **fanatic** about the Aurora Borealis, helped me plan. Manuel had a heart of gold. Whenever anyone new came to town, he was the first to help.

"You want to impress Joe? Well, I'll give it my best try," he told me.

One cold January night, Joe was ready to pounce on anyone and anything. "So you have some lights in the sky?" His voice grew louder as he told us about the nighttime view from the windows of his city apartment. "Nothing can compare to city lights," he bragged.

continued on next page

advantage *n.*, something positive about a place
fanatic *n.*, extreme fan

1. I think in the sticks means:

2. I think chip on his shoulder means:

3. I think had a heart of gold means:

4. I think ready to pounce means:

Natural Lights, continued

To him, our sky was just a dark nothingness. He didn't know how to appreciate natural wonders like the Aurora Borealis. I wanted to say something. Instead, I bit my tongue. No words would convince him.

We walked out to a high ridge. Joe kept complaining about the boring darkness. Manuel tried very hard to liven things up. He started to tell some legends about Aurora Borealis. One was about a boy who whistled to draw the Northern Lights closer to Earth.

Just then the sky began to glow. A bright arc of green speared along the horizon. The ghostly light spread in brilliant rays until the whole sky was covered in **luminous** waves. I looked at Joe. He was **awestruck,** staring at the sky. "Now," I thought, "he's going to have to eat his words."

luminous *adj.*, glowing
awestruck *adj.*, amazed

5. I think bit my tongue means:

6. I think eat his words means:

Review your predictions. Check the ones that make sense. Look the others up in a dictionary and revise the prediction.

Idiom	Does It Make Sense?
1. in the sticks	❑ Yes. It makes sense. ❑ No. I need to use a dictionary.
2. chip on his shoulder	❑ Yes. It makes sense. ❑ No. I need to use a dictionary.
3. had a heart of gold	❑ Yes. It makes sense. ❑ No. I need to use a dictionary.

Idiom	Does It Make Sense?
4. ready to pounce	❑ Yes. It makes sense. ❑ No. I need to use a dictionary.
5. bit my tongue	❑ Yes. It makes sense. ❑ No. I need to use a dictionary.
6. eat his words	❑ Yes. It makes sense. ❑ No. I need to use a dictionary.

Talk About It

Tell a classmate how you figured out the meanings of the idioms.

Make the Ideas Your Own

What is the writer's message in this story? How does it apply to your life?

Name ____________________ Date __________

Similes and Metaphors

Read "An Underground Army." Each underlined phrase makes a comparison. Think about its meaning.

Strategy at a Glance

Go Beyond the Literal Meaning

When you read a **simile** or **metaphor**, ask yourself:

- What two things are being compared?
- How are the two things alike?

DID YOU KNOW?

- Terra cotta is a type of ceramic used for pottery.
- The first emperor of China was Qin Shi Huang.

An Underground Army

In ancient China, an emperor was buried with a life-size army. Two thousand years later, in 1974, peasants found pottery near his tomb. The news was like a gift to people interested in Chinese history. Archaeologists found ceramic soldiers that are now known as the Terra Cotta Warriors. The army stands in battle formation with clay horses and bronze weapons.

The Terra Cotta Warriors are a window into ancient Chinese military strategy. The site is so big, the Emperor Qin Terra Cotta Museum was built over it. Inside, the **excavating** continues.

The Terra Cotta Warriors

excavating *v.*, digging at an archaeological site

Now complete the chart to explain the meaning of each phrase.

Phrase	What Is Being Compared?	How Are They Alike?	How Does the Comparison Help You Understand the Text?
1. The phrase "The news was like a gift" is a ❑ simile ❑ metaphor			
2. The phrase "The Terra Cotta Warriors are a window into" is a ❑ simile ❑ metaphor			

As you read "A Key to the Past," think about the meaning of each underlined phrase. Then complete the chart.

DID YOU KNOW?

- Archaeologists study buildings, tools, and other artifacts to learn about past cultures.

A KEY TO THE PAST

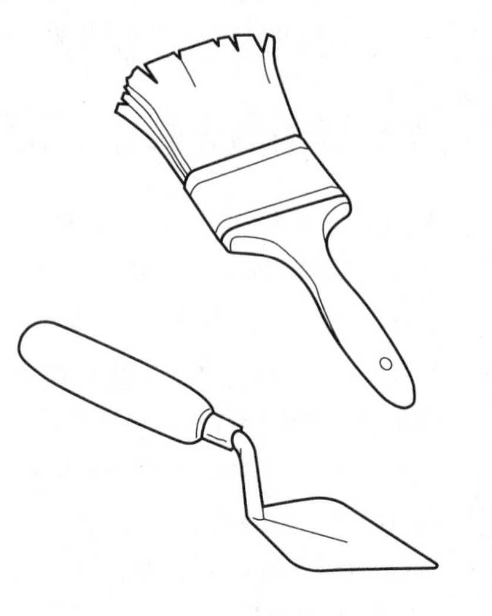

Juliana showed Kripa, her dig partner, the **artifact**. Seeing just another shard of pottery, Kripa shrugged. The archaeology camp was almost over, and she had hoped to discover more. Her spirits were like a deflated balloon.

Kripa dug the earth with a trowel, and picked up a small brush. Spotting a glint of metal, Juliana gasped. Kripa brushed at it and the shape of a key began to emerge. Cool as a cucumber, she continued to dig around the key. Her tired bones didn't matter. She could dig for hours on the chance that she might find what the key would open.

artifact *n.*, an object with historical importance

Phrase	What Is Being Compared?	How Are They Alike?	How Does the Comparison Help You Understand the Text?
3. The phrase "Her spirits were like a deflated balloon" is a ❑ simile ❑ metaphor			
4. The phrase "Cool as a cucumber" is a ❑ simile ❑ metaphor			

Talk About It

Compare your chart with a partner's and discuss how the similes and metaphors helped to create pictures in your mind.

Make the Ideas Your Own

How would you compare the two passages on pages 19 and 20?

Name ______________________ Date __________

Personification

Read "A New Journey" once. Then read it a second time and circle examples of personification.

Strategy at a Glance

Go Beyond the Literal Meaning

When writers use **personification** they give human qualities to nonhuman things.

When you come across personification,

- picture the image in your mind
- think about the meaning.

DID YOU KNOW?

- Egyptians sailed to Punt 4,000 years ago.
- Punt was probably where Eritrea or Yemen is now.

A New Journey

Around the Red Sea

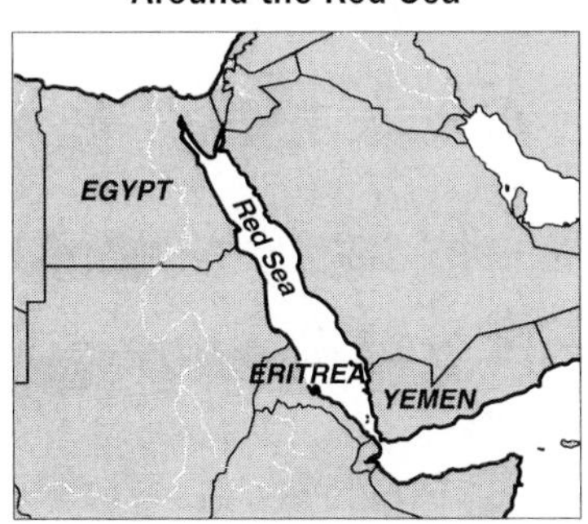

Sweat poured down Rami's and Wati's faces. The army had been **trudging** across the desert carrying ship parts for two days. The desert greeted them with sandstorms and blistering heat. Thousands of **comrades** were moving heavy wooden planks and supplies to the Red Sea's shores. The desert swallowed them as though they were tiny ants. Food and water were the army's only friends.

The sea called Rami like an older brother, leading him to adventure. But Wati feared the sea. "We're river folk, Rami."

After ten days, the men reached the Red Sea port and began **assembling** the ships. One morning, the enormous task was done. The two friends waited as the commander selected the crews. Wati was filled with dread. Rami was bursting with hope.

Luck smiled on them both. Wati and other soldiers would return across the desert, **bearing** a lighter load. Rami would join a crew and sail for Punt. The boys clasped arms in farewell, not knowing if they would ever meet again.

---

trudging *v.*, hiking
comrades *n.*, friends and coworkers
assembling *v.*, putting together
bearing *v.*, carrying

Complete the chart to analyze the writer's use of personification.

Object	Human Quality	Meaning
1.		
2.		
3.		
4.		
5.		

Talk About It

Compare your chart with a classmate's.

Make the Ideas Your Own

As you read the story, what did you picture in your mind?

Name ______________________ Date __________

Use Memory Tips

Read each paragraph. Then use the memory tip to help you remember the meaning of the underlined word.

Like most of our neighbors, we lost our home and our car in the hurricane. Sympathetic people from all over the country sent donations and offered to help rebuild our community.

▶ **Memory Tip: Store It!**
Make a word map for the word. Use a dictionary to check the information in your map.

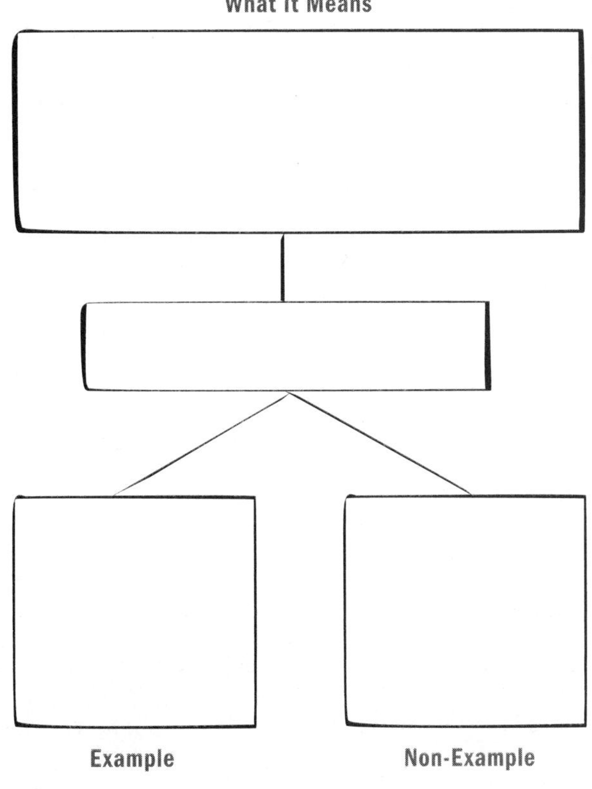

That night a TV news reporter visited the destroyed neighborhoods. More than 246 families lost their homes. "What a horrific scene," whispered the reporter, shaking her head.

▶ **Memory Tip: Explore the Word Family**
Write the word you want to remember. Circle the base word or root. Then make a list of words that share the base word or root. Write a sentence for each word in the family.

Word Family

Sentences:

The levees were weak but they held back the water from the rising seas. If they hadn't been there, builders wouldn't have had an inch of dry land to construct buildings on! Now it was time to <u>fortify</u> the levees.

▶ **Memory Tip: Picture It!**
Use a key word and picture to remember the word *fortify.*

What I think *fortify* means:

____

____

A key word that sounds like the new word:

____

Now make a picture that links the meanings.

When Stephie Sarto began to report on the hurricane for the TV news, she thought all hope was lost for the victims and their ruined dreams. But after more than twenty interviews, she had a different <u>perspective</u>. People were dreaming new dreams.

▶ **Memory Tip: Self-Check Spelling**
Follow these steps to learn to spell the underlined word.

1. Say the word **perspective**.
2. Write the word, syllable-by-syllable.
3. Read what you've written. Does it look and sound right? If not, check the spelling in a dictionary.
4. Repeat steps 1 and 2 three more times.

A hurricane in action

Name ______________________ Date __________

Use Self-Stick Notes

Read "Small Animals with Secret Weapons." Note your questions and comments.

DID YOU KNOW?

- Clever species of animals often outlive others.
- Scientists study animal communication to help protect endangered species.

Small Animals with Secret Weapons

Prairie dog sentries sound warnings of danger.

"Watch out!" a man yells to a boy about to step in front of a car. "Bridge Closed," a sign warns motorists. "Winter storm watch for the next forty-eight hours," the TV news reporter announces. Humans rely on language to stay safe. Some animals behave in ways that are astonishingly similar.

Prairie Dog Lingo

In the grasslands of western North America, up to 250 prairie dogs live together in underground villages. The animals in these communities rely on communication. Their barks, whines, churring, and tooth-clicking may sound like **gibberish** to us. But they are the prairie dogs' language.

So, what are these cooperative animals saying? Scientists have **catalogued** many of their sounds. Their "yip-yip" is a general alarm bark. A more urgent, higher-pitched alarm is the "danger-in-the-sky" signal. To say "all-clear," prairie dogs bark. To show displeasure, they make a soft, growling sound. Young gophers **whimper** when they are afraid. Females chatter their teeth to warn others to stay away from their nests.

One of the marvels of prairie dog behavior is communication through **sentries**. Usually four male sentries are on duty. Each sentry sits upright and faces a different direction. They call warnings whenever danger threatens. The rest of the community goes about their business in safety. They know that a warning will sound if danger approaches.

continued on next page

gibberish *n.,* nonsense
catalogued *v.,* heard and recorded
whimper *v.,* cry softly
sentries *n.,* guards

Write a question.

Write a comment.

Trap what you want to remember.

Continue to read and note your questions and comments.

Small Animals with Secret Weapons, continued

The diana monkey of the Ivory Coast in Africa

Monkey and Hornbill Alert System

Some animals have even learned to **translate** what other species are saying. In some cases, animals that are able to understand other animals' language help one another survive in the wild. A fascinating example is the diana monkey. These troops of monkeys share a jungle environment with leopards and crowned eagles. Those animals are their two main predators. Flocks of hornbills often feed in the same trees as these monkeys. Both the birds and the monkeys fear attacks by crowned eagles.

Diana monkeys give a specific cry of alarm when they spot one of these enemies. Nearby, the yellow-casqued hornbills are **eavesdropping**. The hornbills understand the monkeys' "crowned eagle" alarm call and come to the rescue. They screech and fly around, doing their best to drive the eagle away.

Animals like prairie dogs, hornbills, and diana monkeys are not the largest or strongest creatures in the wild, yet they defend themselves well. What can we learn from the "survival of the communicators"?

---

translate *v.,* understand another language
eavesdropping *v.,* listening in

Write a question.

Write a comment.

Trap what you want to remember.

Make the Ideas Your Own

Review all your notes. Write what you will take away from reading the text.

Name ______________________ Date ____________

Mark the Text

Read "Ode to DNA" once. Then read it again, marking the text to help you focus on what you want to remember.

DID YOU KNOW?

- DNA contains instructions that tell cells how to develop.
- Every living thing contains DNA in its cells.

ODE TO DNA

—Alexandra Phillips

Strange patterned strand
Winding through each cell
Carrying the message of me.

Marching orders for every unit
Meticulously matched,
Dictating the details of me.

Constantly **replicating**,
Repeating in endless copies,
The physical essence of me.

Oblivious to will or emotion,
Innocent of consequences,
Calmly repeating me, me, me…

continued on next page

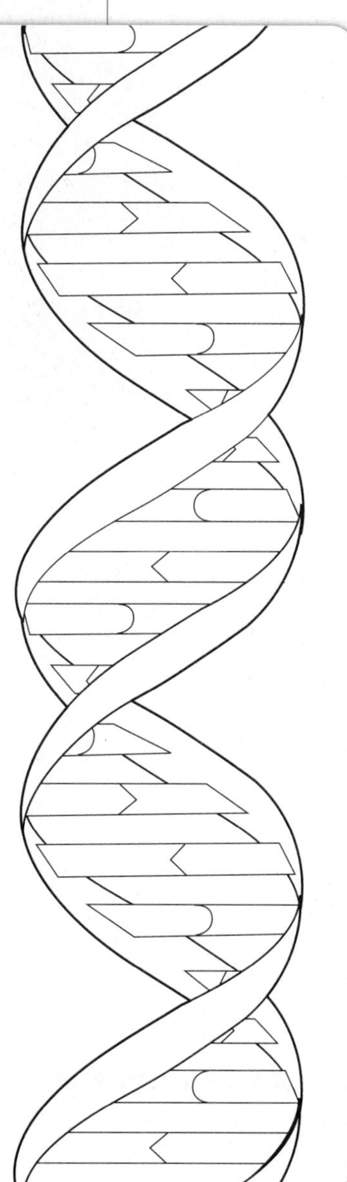

meticulously *adv.*, carefully and in great detail
replicating *v.*, making copies
oblivious *adj.*, knowing nothing about something

Mark the Text, continued

Continue marking the text as you read the poem.

Ode to DNA, continued

Indecipherable maze,
Unpronounceable name,
Complex identity of me.

No two alike, some twins excepted,
In millions of human kind.
One designs only me.

Etchings of my presence,
Each step of the journey
Marked by me.

Every deed recorded,
For good or ill, in
Tell-tale traces of me.

Comprising a half-**legacy**,
For my offspring.
The elegant perfection of me.

---

indecipherable *adj.*, can't be figured out
comprising *v.*, making up, containing
legacy *n.*, what one generation passes on to the next

Look back at your notes. What do you want to remember?

Make the Ideas Your Own
What makes each person unique? Is it DNA, or other things?
Explain your answer.

Name ______________________ Date __________

Expand the Conversation

Preview "Spawning" so that you know what to expect when you read. Read the poem once. Then read it again, marking the text with your questions and comments.

DID YOU KNOW?

- Salmon lay eggs in freshwater streams and riverbeds.
- They return to their birthplaces to create the next generation.

Spawning

—Thomas Jackelwood

We head home
Across the dark, salty seas,
Against the mighty **current**
Gleaming and silver
Swimming as one.

Packed tight together,
Scaring off danger,
We know the way
Up the cold, fresh river.
Battling upstream.

We soar over rapids,
Leap over waterfalls,
We make our way back—
Back to our riverbed.
Destined for our birthplace.

Our young **hatch** in the freshwater
Grow strong and **lithe**
In the flow of the stream—then
Away, as generations before,
Swimming to the open sea.

Our brown striped young
Now darting silver bullets
Disguised in the sea and free
As we once were,
Not yet journeying home.

But one day answering a call,
Leaving saltwater, seeking fresh
Swimming the vast sea miles
Finding their birth river, and now
Spawning life again.

---

current *n.,* flow of water
gleaming *adj.,* shiny
hatch *v.,* are born
lithe *adj.,* graceful
spawning *v.,* creating

Use your notes to complete the chart. Exchange pages with a classmate to see if you both reacted the same way.

Student 1:	Student 2:
I think the poet's message is:	I think the poet's message is:
My Questions:	My Questions:
What I want to remember:	What I want to remember:
My Personal Connections:	My Personal Connections:

Make the Ideas Your Own

Which images in the poem stand out? What lessons does the poem teach about human nature?

Name ____________________ Date __________

Keep a Journal or Log

Preview "Picturing Our Planet—2050" so that you know what to expect when you read. As you read the essay, use the chart to record what the writer says and your own thoughts and feelings.

DID YOU KNOW?

- The U.S. and China are the world's biggest air polluters.
- More than one million plants and animals may become extinct due to global warming.

Picturing Our Planet—2050

Try to picture what our planet will look like in 2050. Some see a world where stronger hurricanes hit more often than ever before. Deadly diseases like malaria are widespread. Melting glaciers raise the sea level. The coastal states of New York and Florida are underwater. They see **drastic** changes in our natural world that occur as the result of global warming.

Carbon dioxide (CO_2) traps heat in the atmosphere.

The earth's atmosphere is made up of greenhouse gases. These gases trap the sun's heat. This keeps the planet warm. Burning fossil fuels like coal, gas, and oil adds gases to the atmosphere. Every day, people add more and more gases, specifically carbon dioxide, to the air. The more carbon dioxide that gets into the atmosphere, the hotter it gets.

continued on next page

drastic *adj.*, extreme

What the Text Says	What I Think, Feel, and Know

Continue reading and recording your thoughts and feelings.

Picturing Our Planet—2050, continued

Now **envision** a new way to live, starting now. People move to undo the damage. They cut down fewer trees. How does this help? Trees absorb carbon dioxide from the air. In fact, a single tree can absorb a ton of carbon dioxide throughout its life. Think of how much a whole forest can absorb! Yet, forests are being cut down quickly. Now, more than a dozen nations with rainforests are working **jointly** to find other options. These countries will **retain** their natural resources for their own communities. And they may save the entire planet as well.

Individuals cannot wait for nations to act, experts say. Here's what individuals can do. Wash clothes in cold or warm water instead of hot. Unplug unneeded appliances and recycle glass and paper. These are simple actions that have a dramatic impact.

Does the vision of an improved future come into focus now? By working together and as individuals, you and all citizens of Earth can make that picture a reality in 2050.

Destruction of forests in the Amazon in Brazil

---

envision *v.,* imagine
jointly *adv.,* together
retain *v.,* keep

What the Text Says	What I Think, Feel, and Know

Make the Ideas Your Own

Has this article changed your thinking in any way? What did you learn about global warming?

Name ______________________ Date ____________

Preview

Preview "Marco Polo: Adventurer." What is the topic? How do you know?

____

____

____

Now preview the passage to figure out the major genre. Use this checklist:

Strategy at a Glance

Plan Your Reading

When you preview, you

- take a quick look at what you're about to read
- look at the title, headings, pictures, and any boldface words
- figure out the topic
- figure out the major type of writing, or genre.

Fiction	Nonfiction
Look for these elements: ❑ imaginary events and conflicts ❑ characters who use dialogue ❑ a real or imaginary setting ❑ illustrations or photographs	Look for these elements: ❑ facts about real people and events ❑ headings, subheadings, and words in bold type ❑ key information in photos, graphics, and captions

DID YOU KNOW?

- Paper money had not been invented in the 13th century.
- Sometimes Europeans used spices as money.

Marco Polo: Adventurer

Marco Sets Out

Marco Polo wasn't like other teenagers in 1271. At seventeen, he left Venice, Italy, to start his great **exploration** of Asia. Polo spent the next 24 years traveling the Silk Road. This traders' **route** wound through China, India, and the Middle East.

Marco's Lessons

In China, Marco met the great ruler Kublai Khan. Polo stayed in China serving Khan for many years. He finally returned to Venice in 1295. He brought back spices, riches, and stories of his travels. He taught the Western World about the wonders that lie east of Europe.

Marco Polo's Travels

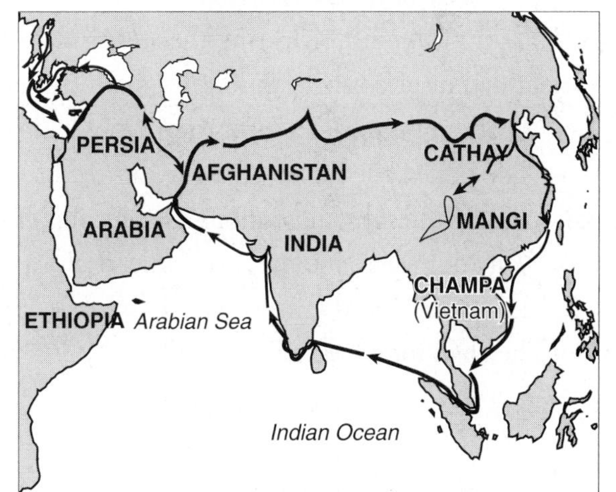

exploration *n.,* travel to new areas
route *n.,* path

Preview "Silk Road Troubles." What is the topic? How do you know?

Now preview the passage to figure out the major genre. Use this checklist:

Fiction	Nonfiction
Look for these elements: ❑ imaginary events and conflicts ❑ characters who use dialogue ❑ a real or imaginary setting ❑ illustrations or photographs	Look for these elements: ❑ facts about real people and events ❑ headings, subheadings, and words in bold type ❑ key information in photos, graphics, and captions

DID YOU KNOW?

- It took almost a year to travel the whole Silk Road.
- Sandstorms, ice storms, and lack of water made the Silk Road very dangerous.

Silk Road Troubles

Nicholas saw a dark cloud in the desert sky.

"We need rain, Christopher," he said. They had been traveling the Silk Road for months. Hearing the stories of Marco Polo's travels to the **Orient** had inspired them to seek similar fortunes.

"That's not rain. It's a sandstorm!" cried Christopher. "Take cover!"

They pulled the fabric off their camels' backs and hid as winds and sand blasted the silks and cottons. Before long, it was quiet again.

"Why did we ever come here?" said Nicholas.

"That's why," said Christopher as an **oasis** appeared on the horizon. They had found a trading town!

Orient *n.*, countries of eastern Asia
oasis *n.*, place with water in the desert

Talk About It

Tell your teacher or a classmate how you figured out the topic and major genre of each selection.

Name ______________________ Date ____________

Make Predictions

Preview "John Muir: Pioneer Naturalist." Then make predictions before and during your reading.

Strategy at a Glance

Plan and Monitor Your Reading

When you make predictions, you

- think about the topic and genre
- add what you already know about the topic
- predict, or think about what you will learn, as you read
- confirm or revise your prediction as you find new information.

DID YOU KNOW?

- In the 1800s, there were no roads or travelers' services in most of the western U.S.
- Most of the West had never been explored.

1. Preview and connect to what you know.

   Topic: ______________________

   Genre: ______________________

   What I know about the topic:

   ____

2. Make your first prediction.

   I will learn: ______________________

3. As you read, look for new information and confirm or revise your prediction.

   New Information: ______________________

   New Prediction: ______________________

John Muir: Pioneer Naturalist

John Muir in the Sierras

A Life-Changing Accident

In 1867, a young man named John Muir had a terrible accident. He was temporarily blinded working at a **carriage** shop. The accident seemed to inspire Muir. He **resolved** to follow his dream. He decided to explore as much of the world as he could. First he walked 1,000 miles from Indianapolis to the Gulf of Mexico. From there he continued westward to California.

The Maverick Explorer

Muir soon developed amazing survival skills. All he brought to the mountains was a sack full of tea and dried bread. When it rained, he climbed trees and slept in their branches. Leaves and pine needles served as his sleeping bag.

continued on next page

carriage *n.*, wheeled vehicle pulled by horses
resolved *v.*, decided

4. Continue looking for new information. Revise your prediction.

New Information: ____________

____

____

____

New Prediction: ____________

____

____

____

Talk About It

Tell your teacher or a classmate about your predictions and how you confirmed and revised them as you read.

Make the Ideas Your Own

What did you learn about John Muir from this article?

____

____

____

____

____

____

____

____

____

____

____

____

John Muir: Pioneer Naturalist, continued

Discovering the Glaciers

The Muir Glacier, named after John Muir

In 1879, Muir took a steamship to Alaska. He wanted to search for glaciers in the Alaskan wilderness. At Fort Wrangell he joined a group of native people. They were traveling north in a canoe. One rainy Sunday, most of the group sat around the fire in camp. Muir climbed 1,460 feet to the top of a nearby **ridge**. He saw something amazing from this view. No white explorer had ever seen the sight before.

This first glimpse of Glacier Bay captivated John Muir. He sat in a protected **crevasse** and made notes. He also sketched the landscape. "The clouds lifted a little," he wrote. "Beneath their fringes I saw the berg-filled expanse of the bay, and the feet of the mountains that stand about it and the **imposing** fronts of five huge glaciers."

Muir returned to explore Glacier Bay several more times. Each voyage was dangerous work. He jumped wide crevasses. He had to cross shaky ice bridges. He worked alone for twelve to fourteen hours a day. He took notes and absorbed all he could of the area.

Go! Go and See

Muir used his notes to write articles for a San Francisco newspaper. He urged others to experience the spectacular beauty of the Alaskan landscape. His writing informed people about conserving nature and inspired them. Even now Muir's writings draw people to the Alaskan wilderness. He helped the world understand the value of "Seward's Icebox."

---

ridge *n.,* chain of mountains
crevasse *n.,* deep crack or opening
imposing *adj.,* large and awesome

Name ____________________ Date __________

Set a Purpose: Fiction

Preview "Race to the Finish" to set a purpose for reading. Then read the story.

Strategy at a Glance

Plan Your Reading

When you set a purpose for reading fiction, you

- decide what you look forward to finding out.

DID YOU KNOW?

- NASCAR stands for the National Association for Stock Car Auto Racing.
- In NASCAR races, speeds can exceed 200 mph.

1. Preview and set your purpose.

   How I know this is fiction:

   ____

   ____

   ____

   ____

   ____

   What I want to find out:

   ____

   ____

   ____

   ____

   ____

2. Keep your purpose in mind as you read the story. Collect details that go with your purpose.

   Details that connect to my purpose:

   ____

   ____

   ____

   ____

   ____

   ____

RACE TO THE FINISH

NASCAR drivers speeding into a turn

Darrell's dream of being a NASCAR hero came down to the wire. Only one car ahead of him, and Cassie was in the driver's seat. He was amazed at the speed and agility she showed. She could **maneuver** her car in and out of the crowded lanes easily. She was beating every man out there—so far. Darrell was determined. He pushed his **accelerator,** ignoring his **pit crew** waving him in. He'd seen Cassie get waved in. Now was his chance to make up for lost time.

A smile edged across his face. One lap to go. He could see the crowd in his mind cheering, smiling, waving, and shouting his name. He'd be a hero, with two NASCAR wins, and—what!? Darrell couldn't believe what he saw. Cassie was edging back out onto the track. If he didn't do something soon, he'd lose the race.

"Oh, no, no!" thought Darrell. "This can't be happening!"

continued on next page

---

maneuver *v.*, skillfully operate
accelerator *n.*, gas pedal
pit crew *n.*, race car mechanics

3. Keep your purpose in mind as you read the rest of the story. Keep track of story details that connect with your purpose.

Details that connect to my purpose:

____

____

____

____

____

More details I want to remember:

____

____

____

____

4. Did you achieve your purpose for reading? Why or why not?

____

____

____

____

____

____

Make the Ideas Your Own

What did you learn from reading the story?

____

____

____

____

Race to the Finish, continued

Darrell raced forward and eased his car next to Cassie's. Out of the corner of his eye, he saw her glance his way. Darrell wanted to make sure she knew he hadn't gone away. He was going to win this race no matter what. Darrell stared straight ahead and floored the accelerator. Cassie's car was keeping pace with his as they sped toward the checkered flag.

"She can't win," Darrell said aloud. "She can't!"

Both racers slipped and slid down the oily raceway. Suddenly, Darrell's car began to slide toward the outer wall. He gripped the steering wheel as his car swung dangerously right, then left. He could see Cassie's car attempting to avoid a **collision** with his. Darrell had to gain control of his vehicle. Suddenly he felt the back right wheel come loose. He watched it race past him and hit the wall. He had to slow down! Other cars whizzed past, trying to avoid his damaged vehicle. When he finally came to a stop, he heard the crowd let out a cheer. Darrell dropped his head in anguish when he realized the cheer was not for him. Cassie had won the race, and although Darrell was disappointed, he congratulated her on winning an amazing race.

---

collision *n.,* car accident

Name ______________________ Date __________

Set a Purpose: Nonfiction

Preview "Climbing Blind" to set a purpose for reading. Then read the article.

Strategy at a Glance

Plan Your Reading

When you set a purpose for reading nonfiction, you

- predict what new information you will learn from the text
- decide what facts to look for while you read.

DID YOU KNOW?

- Mt. Everest is the world's tallest mountain.
- It is located near India and China.
- Every mountain climber dreams of climbing it.

1. Preview and set your purpose.

   Topic: ______________________

   What I want to learn from the text: ______________________

2. Keep your purpose in mind as you read. Collect important facts.

   Important facts: ______________________

Climbing Blind

Himalaya Mountains, Nepal-Tibet border

Imagine climbing to the highest spot on Earth. You made your way through enormous boulders. You crossed frozen narrow ice bridges and inched across massive **glaciers**. Now you are at the top of Mt. Everest, on the Nepal-Tibet border. You are gasping for breath in the thin air. At 29,000 feet above sea level, there is only one-third the normal amount of oxygen. The wind is howling and the temperature can drop to –30° F (–34° C).

Now imagine you're standing in the icy coldness and you cannot see anything at all. That's the experience of blind mountain climber Erik Weihenmayer. In 2001, Erik became the first blind person to reach the **summit** of the "top of the world"—Mount Everest. He was part of a team of 18 climbers, including a climber leader.

Erik lost his sight when he was 13 years old. He went to a center where he learned to use a cane to get

continued on next page

glaciers *n.,* large areas of moving ice
summit *n.,* top of a mountain

3. Keep your purpose in mind as you continue to read. Keep track of new information that connects with your purpose.

Information that connects to my purpose:

____

____

____

____

____

____

____

____

____

____

____

____

Talk About It

Tell your teacher or a classmate about your purpose for reading and the new information you learned.

Make the Ideas Your Own

What did you learn about Erik Weihenmayer from reading the selection?

____

____

____

____

____

____

Climbing Blind, continued

around. He also learned to read using Braille. Eventually Erik felt that he could do all the things he used to do, if he just looked for a different way to do them.

Erik Weihenmayer on Mt. Everest

That was when Erik started rock climbing. He learned to climb with his hands and his feet, instead of with his eyes. He used his hands and feet to find the next place to hold. He practiced and practiced. Eventually Erik started thinking about climbing big mountains.

After years of climbing, Erik thought he was ready for Mt. Everest. He created a team that would work with him. Erik said later, "The idea of this wasn't just to drag a blind guy to the summit... The idea was to create an **integrated** team, one of whom happens to be blind, a team where everyone contributes to the overall success of the team."

And that's what they did. Erik created special hiking and climbing techniques. He used two long poles to "feel" the **terrain** ahead, and he followed the sound of bells attached to the leader's pack. As Erik's team neared the summit, most of their climb had to be done in the dark. The **sighted** climbers had great difficulty—but not Erik. His strong climbing helped everyone get to the top. Erik says, "When I stood on the top, I knew that I wasn't just standing there alone with my team, but I was standing there on the shoulders of thousands and thousands of people all around the world."

---

integrated *adj.,* working together as a whole
terrain *n.,* ground
sighted *adj.,* able to see

Name ______________________ Date ____________

Tap Into the Text Structure

Preview the passages on pages 41–42. Which graphic organizer shows how the text is organized? Write the title of the passage in the chart.

Strategy at a Glance

Plan Your Reading

When you tap into the text structure, you

- preview to figure out the topic and genre
- notice how the writer organized the ideas and information.

Text Structure	Graphic Organizer	Passage
Narrative	Goal-and-Outcome Map Goal → Obstacles → Strategies → Outcome	Title:
Time Order	Time Line Beginning, Event, Event, End	Title:
Compare and Contrast	Venn Diagram What the writer says / What I think	Title:

Now read each passage, keeping the organization in mind.

An Aviation Pioneer

Amelia Earhart was the first woman pilot to cross the Atlantic Ocean in a plane. That was in 1928. The flight was a pioneering event in aviation history. Earhart became a national hero. Nine years later, Amelia tried to be the first woman to fly around the world, but her plane disappeared over the Pacific Ocean.

Amelia Earhart prepares to fly.

Heroes or Thrill Seekers?

By Alex Bateman

Some people believe that stunt pilots are heroes. Like our military pilots, they have excellent flying skills. But do they really deserve our admiration? I believe that stunt pilots are reckless thrill seekers. They fly for money, not to protect our country. Both stunt pilots and military pilots risk injury and even death. Should we encourage such risk for entertainment?

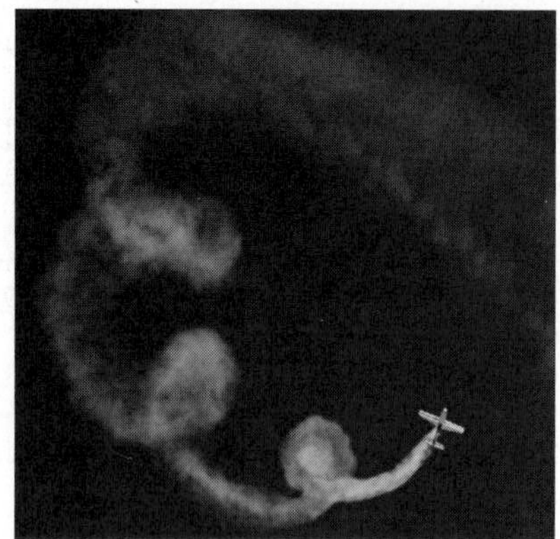

A stunt pilot shows off

Maverick in the Sky

The farmers and their families cheered with excitement.

After flying dangerously low over the surrounding barns, Teresa James shot high into the sky. At the peak of her ascent, the plane rolled back and began to fall.

The crowd started counting, "One, two . . ." A death-defying trick! "Sixteen, seventeen . . ." The stunt was making Teresa dizzy. "Twenty-five. TWENTY-SIX!" She had done it. Twenty-six spinning turns in midair was a new record!

Talk About It

Tell your teacher or a classmate how you tapped into the text structure of each passage.

Make the Ideas Your Own

What do you think about pilots who take risks? Explain your answer?

Name ______________________ Date ____________

Ask Yourself Questions

Preview "Young, Smart, and Published" so that you know what to expect when you read. As you read, use the self-stick notes to ask and answer questions about the writer's words and ideas. If you found the answer, tell if you reread or read on.

Strategy at a Glance

Monitor Your Reading

When you ask yourself questions, you

- pause now and then to make sure you understand the text
- reread or read on to clear up confusing parts.

DID YOU KNOW?

- Many authors get published in magazines first.
- Authors who write a lot of books can make a good living writing.

Young, Smart, and Published

How would you like to get a check for $460,000? That's how much some people say a new author received after showing a publisher a mere 80 pages. Who is this amazing author? She's the young British writer, Zadie Smith.

The publisher, Hamish Hamilton, placed a large bet on this young author. He won big! Zadie was just 24 when her first book, *White Teeth*, became a **bestseller**. The book earned many awards, too.

Zadie was young, confident, and intelligent. How was she able to write so well at such a young age? Smith is quick to point out. "The best, the only training you can get is from reading other people's books," Smith adds. "I read everything I could get my hands on."

Zadie Smith, bestselling author

bestseller *n.*, very popular book

1.

To find the answer, I

- ❏ reread
- ❏ read on

2.

To find the answer, I

- ❏ reread
- ❏ read on

3.

To find the answer, I

- ❏ reread
- ❏ read on

Preview "An Inside Look at *The Outsiders*" so that you know what to expect when you read. As you read, use the self-stick notes to ask and answer questions about the writer's words and ideas. If you found the answer, tell if you reread or read on.

An Inside Look at *The Outsiders*

Greasers were the rebels of S.E. Hinton's day.

Susan Eloise Hinton became successful at an early age. Hinton began writing her most famous book, *The Outsiders,* while she was still a student in her Oklahoma high school.

The social divisions among her schoolmates **aggravated** Hinton. The situation also **motivated** her to start writing. *The Outsiders* featured Ponyboy Curtis, a 14-year-old greaser. Ponyboy watched his friend, Johnny, kill a rich kid from school.

In 1967, boys didn't read books by women. Susan said, "I figured that most boys would look at the book and think, 'What can a chick know about stuff like that?'" She decided to write under the name S.E. Hinton. The **pseudonym** worked. For years, many young male readers would write letters to "Mr. Hinton."

There are more than eight million copies of *The Outsiders* in print today. It is one of the best-selling books for young adults in publishing history. The book was made into a film. The film starred several young actors who would later become stars.

---

aggravated *v.*, frustrated
motivated *v.*, caused to take action
pseudonym *n.*, false name

1.

To find the answer, I
- ❑ reread
- ❑ read on

2.

To find the answer, I
- ❑ reread
- ❑ read on

3.

To find the answer, I
- ❑ reread
- ❑ read on

Talk About It

Talk with your teacher or a classmate about questions you asked, how you found answers, and any questions you could not answer.

Name ______________________ Date ______________

Make Connections to Your Life

Preview "Young Entrepreneurs" so that you know what to expect when you read. As you read, make connections to your life.

Strategy at a Glance

Monitor Your Reading

To make connections to your life, you

- think about what your life has taught you about the topic
- ask if the text makes sense with what you know
- think about your experiences in similar situations.

DID YOU KNOW?

- Entrepreneurs start or manage new businesses.
- Entrepreneurs are willing to take risks to meet their goals.

What my life has taught me about the topic: ______________________

____

____

____

____

____

The text makes sense because

____

____

____

____

____

My experiences in similar situations: ______________________

____

____

____

____

____

____

____

____

Young Entrepreneurs

B-r-i-n-g! It's the lunch bell. Thank goodness. You're starved. Too bad the cafeteria choices are less than wonderful: a leathery slice of pizza, a corndog, or tuna casserole.

Of course, you've wished there were better food to eat. But have you ever **considered** doing something about it?

At Santa Monica High School, somebody did—the students! Instead of going along with the cafeteria herd, a group of students became lunchroom pioneers. They turned a little-used teachers' lounge into Vike's Café, a student-run café focused on serving food that's a little healthier than the typical cafeteria food. The café has a walk-up window that is open during lunch five days a week.

It takes 15 students to run Vike's Café daily. The business serves over 246 students per day. Menu changes were based on health and quality. For example, they added a Chicken Caesar Salad with low-fat dressing. They switched pizza **vendors** because they weren't satisfied with the quality. In a far more dramatic change, Vike's now bakes rather than fries everything, from potato fries to popcorn chicken.

continued on next page

---

considered *v.,* thought about

vendors *n.,* sellers

What my life has taught me about the topic: ______________

____

____

____

____

____

The text makes sense because

____

____

____

____

____

My experiences in similar situations: ______________

____

____

____

____

Young Entrepreneurs, continued

Vike's café took first place in the Students for the Advancement of Global Entrepreneurship (SAGE) USA Competition. The Santa Monica team will go on to the SAGE World Cup event where they will compete with teams from ten different countries around the world. The competitors are all high school students with a desire to be their own bosses and a plan for doing so. They're pioneers in a big way.

Entrepreneurship, running your own business, is rewarding in many ways. Jon Brennfleck, a college student with his own yard service business, expects to make about $41,000 this year. Being a pioneer can pay.

How does someone learn to be an entrepreneur? One way is by going to college. Quite a few colleges and universities are offering courses in entrepreneurship. And, the training is not merely useful for starting your own business. **Employers** like to hire students who have taken entrepreneurship classes. Students with an entrepreneurial focus can **integrate** successfully into almost any business environment.

College classes can also give you confidence to take the own-your-own-business plunge. Emily Garbardi, a Wilkes University graduate, never even considered owning her own business when she was in high school. After stumbling into the entrepreneur program, Emily is now looking for a business of her own. The entrepreneurial herd is growing, one pioneer at a time. Care to join?

---

employers *n.,* bosses
integrate *v.,* join

Talk About It

Tell your teacher or a classmate about how you connected the text to what you know.

Make the Ideas Your Own

What do you know now about entrepreneurship that you didn't know before?

____

____

____

____

Name ______________________ Date ______________

Picture the Text

Preview "Bethany Hamilton: Surfer Hero" so that you know what to expect when you read. As you read, form pictures in your mind.

Strategy at a Glance

Monitor Your Reading

When you picture the text, you

- use your senses to create mental images of what the writer is describing
- use your experiences to imagine events or characters' feelings.

DID YOU KNOW?

- Tiger sharks sometimes attack surfers in Hawaii.
- Patients who have good attitudes heal quickly.

BETHANY HAMILTON: SURFER HERO

Bethany in action

As she paddled out to catch her first wave of the day on Halloween Day, 2003, Bethany Hamilton had no idea that her life was about to change. To her, surfing was life. The Hawaii native began surfing in competitions when she was just 11 years old. Her dream of becoming a professional surfer was interrupted just two years later. At the age of 13, Bethany was about to face one of the most **horrific** scenes a surfer can imagine.

It was a beautiful morning in Hawaii. The sun was shining and the gulls were flying overhead. Bethany sat on her surfboard in the clear ocean waters off the coast of Kauai's North Shore. Out of nowhere, a 14-foot tiger shark sunk its jagged teeth into her arm. It bit off her arm at the shoulder and then disappeared. Bleeding profusely, Bethany used her right arm to paddle to shore where a friend's father tied a **tourniquet** beneath her shoulder. They rushed her to a local hospital where the doctors were able to save her life.

Would you ever surf again if this happened to you? Bethany didn't quit after her **ordeal**. The doctors said her excellent physical condition enabled her to survive. Not only did she survive, she went back into the ocean to catch another wave. Just months after the nearly fatal accident, she was back on a surfboard and competing in surfing contests. That same year she earned a spot on the U.S. National Surfing Team. She also won an award for Best Comeback Athlete.

continued on next page

horrific *adj.*, frightening and disturbing
tourniquet *n.*, tight bandage use to stop bleeding
ordeal *n.*, very difficult experience

Continue to picture the text as you read.

Bethany Hamilton: Surfer Hero, continued

People around the world read about Bethany's ordeal. They were inspired by her courage and the ease with which she was able to **overcome** her disability. According to Bethany, "People I don't even know come up to me. I guess they see me as a symbol of courage and inspiration. One thing hasn't changed—and that's how I feel when I'm riding a wave. It's like, here I am. I'm still here."

Since her attack, Bethany has won several surfing contests. But surfing is only part of her life now. She has written a book about her experiences and has appeared on many television shows including *Oprah* and the *Tonight Show.* She also travels to cities around the world to speak to groups about the importance of not giving up. In 2005, she visited **disabled** soldiers who had either lost limbs or had been injured during the war in Iraq. Her message was simple: "Me quit? Never."

For Bethany, quitting was never an option.

overcome *v.,* rise above
disabled *adj.,* injured

Complete the chart to show how you used your senses.

Sight	Sound	Smell	Taste	Touch

How I see the events: ____________________

____

____

____

How I imagine the character felt: ____________________

____

____

____

Name ______________________ Date ____________

Explain It in Your Own Words

Preview "Dr. Jonas Salk: Polio Pioneer" so that you know what to expect when you read. Then read the first part of the article.

Strategy at a Glance

Monitor Your Reading

To explain the text, you put the ideas into your own words. You may need to

- break sentences into parts
- read the hard parts slowly
- check a reference or discuss the part with someone.

DID YOU KNOW?

- The poliovirus is a very contagious disease.
- It crippled many children in the early 19th century.

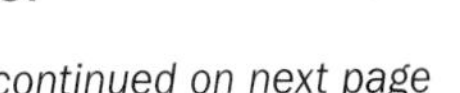

Dr. Jonas Salk: Polio Pioneer

One of the most dreaded diseases of the twentieth century was the poliovirus. It attacked the nervous system and caused **paralysis**. Children were polio's most vulnerable victims. Frightened parents were desperate to protect their children from this incurable disease. Doctors did what they could, but a treatment wasn't found until Jonas Salk pioneered an idea for a polio **vaccine**.

Dr. Jonas Salk

Salk worked with Dr. Thomas Francis at the University of Michigan. He saw first-hand the work Dr. Francis did to treat influenza, or "the flu" for short. They developed the first "killed" influenza vaccine. Instead of using a living virus, the doctors killed the flu virus without destroying it. This experience gave Salk the knowledge he would need to treat polio. All Dr. Salk needed was money for research. Then he could learn how to apply the flu vaccine approach to the poliovirus.

continued on next page

paralysis *n.*, a condition that makes people unable to move
vaccine *n.*, treatment to prevent a disease

Now pause to explain what you read so far in your own words.

What the Text Says	What It Means

Read the rest of the article.

Dr. Jonas Salk: Polio Pioneer, continued

Dr. Salk couldn't have found a more powerful supporter. The President of the United States, Franklin D. Roosevelt, had been crippled by polio. He established a foundation to donate enough money to support Salk's research for the next eight years. Salk employed the same approach Dr. Francis had used to treat the flu. His ideas were new, and most scientists doubted that a "killed" virus would work against polio. In 1950, all Salk's hard work would be tested.

Salk's discovery made national headlines.

First, researchers gave the "killed" vaccine to people who had polio. This test showed that the patients' ability to fight against polio increased. Then, researchers gave more than one million healthy children the vaccine. These children were called the "Polio Pioneers." These pioneers didn't get polio. Tests showed their bodies could now fight off the virus. Salk had created a safe and **effective** vaccine!

Salk's vaccine came when more than 53,000 people had polio in the United States. In the first three years of vaccinating people, the number of polio **cases** dropped by 85 to 90 percent.

Salk was a hero. He received the Congressional Gold Medal of Honor for his work. He also received the highest award for an ordinary citizen, the Presidential Medal of Freedom. Polio is a disease without a cure. But today, thanks to the work of pioneers such as Dr. Salk, polio can be prevented.

---

effective *adj.*, works well
cases *n.*, number of people who have a disease

Now pause to explain this part of the text in your own words.

What the Text Says	What It Means

Talk About It

Ask your teacher or a classmate about parts that are still confusing.

Name ____________________ Date __________

Clarify Vocabulary

Clarify vocabulary as you read "Daring Doctors."

Strategy at a Glance

Monitor Your Reading

To figure out the meaning of an unfamiliar word, you

- think of other words that look like it
- look for clues in the text
- look for word parts
- think about how you can get help.

DID YOU KNOW?

- When a country is at war, it is otten difficult for medical groups to get help to victims.

As you read, circle and clarify unfamiliar words. Then show your thinking here.

1. Unfamiliar Word:

____

I think it means: ____________________

____

____

I figured it out by: ____________________

____

____

2. Unfamiliar Word:

____

I think it means: ____________________

____

____

____

I figured it out by: ____________________

____

____

____

____

Daring Doctors

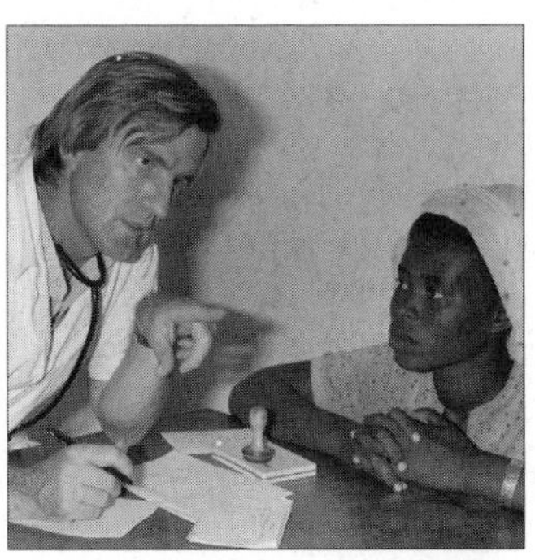

Doctors Without Borders helps millions of people.

In 1969, millions of Africans were caught in the middle of a civil war and faced starvation. Nigeria blocked Red Cross aid to the state of Biafra. The Nigerian Government took charge of the **borders**. It was impossible to get medical assistance. Not many people even cared about the victims in Biafra. Those who did care couldn't do anything to help.

This situation frustrated Dr. Bernard Kouchner. He worked with the Red Cross in Biafra. In 1971, he and a group of concerned medics came up with a plan. They decided to form their own emergency medical team. Their organization would **intervene** with medical aid in any conflict or disaster. They would help wherever they were needed. No government could tell them to leave. It would be a **humanitarian** group with no ties to any government. They call themselves Doctors Without Borders. Their efforts are funded by private donations.

continued on next page

borders *n.,* places where one country ends and another begins

intervene *v.,* take action to help

humanitarian *adj.,* helpful to people

3. Unfamiliar Word: ____________________

I think it means: ____________________

____

____

____

I figured it out by: ____________________

____

____

____

____

4. Unfamiliar Word: ____________________

I think it means: ____________________

____

____

____

I figured it out by: ____________________

____

____

____

____

Talk About It

Talk with your teacher or a classmate about resources you can use to learn about new words in the article.

Daring Doctors, continued

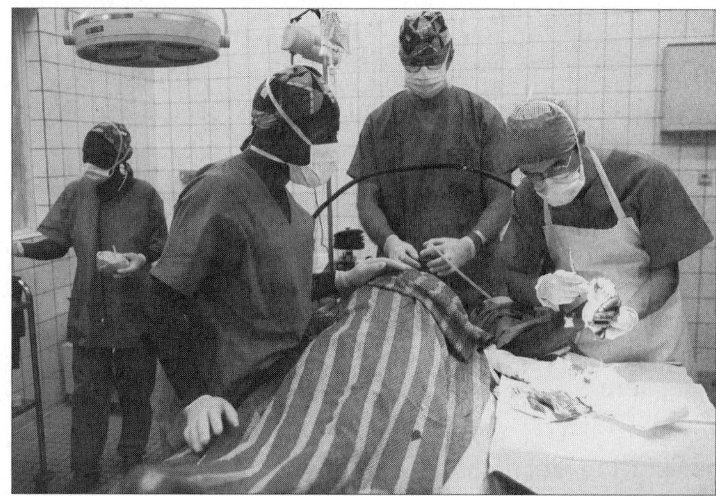

Doctors treat an injured patient.

Doctors Without Borders made a name for itself in the 1970s and 1980s. They drew the world's attention to the horrors of war. Currently, more than 2,000 doctors from 45 countries **volunteer**.

Missions to over 80 countries bring the doctors face to face with dreadful conditions. The risks don't stop the doctors. They continue to open clinics. They also train local people in basic medical care. More medical workers volunteer every day. Aid workers take on a new task when they return home from their mission. Their job is to tell others about the Doctors Without Borders experience.

In 1999, Doctors Without Borders won the Nobel Peace Prize. The prize recognized the organization's work on several continents. It puts action behind Dr. Kauchner's **conviction** that "mankind's suffering belongs to us all."

volunteer *v.*, work without pay
conviction *n.*, strong belief

Name ______________________ Date ____________

Plan and Monitor Your Reading

Before you begin to read, preview the text to get ready for what lies ahead. Preview "A Key Decision" and answer these questions.

1. What are the topic and the genre of this selection?

   Topic: ______________________

   Genre: ______________________

2. What do you want to find out as you read the selection?

   ____

Strategy at a Glance

Plan and Monitor Your Reading

When you plan and monitor your reading, you

- preview, make predictions, and think about your purpose
- check in with yourself to clear up confusing ideas and vocabulary.

Now read the story. As you read, stay in control to get the most out of your reading.

A KEY DECISION

"Most people would not give this away," Addy frowned. "I don't understand how you can even think about it!" She and Vivian sat on the nubby maroon carpeting in Vivian's bedroom, surrounded by colorful **skeins** and metal key rings. They had been working for hours on the key rings Vivian designed.

"I know you want to raise money for William," Addy continued. "But you should keep some of the money as payment for your time and talent. If you don't, you'll never have a successful business."

Vivian held two fistfuls of cash. She counted $2,162. On the outside, she felt confident, but inside she was aching. Two summers ago William Bay had been given a cancer **diagnosis**. William was a seven-year-old kid who lived next door. Vivian had watched him endure two long years of treatment.

continued on next page

skeins *n.,* loosely wound thread
diagnosis *n.,* test that showed he had the disease

Check Your Understanding

3. Why are Vivian and Addy making key rings?

   ____

Plan and Monitor Your Reading, continued

A Key Decision, continued

"I just have to do as much as I can," Vivian sighed. "William and his family have been through so much!"

When William's doctor bills started to **mount**, Vivian decided to help. She had an eye for fashion and a head for business. She organized a successful fundraiser selling hundreds of key rings she designed. Afterwards, she began to make other **accessories**, and now she was making a profit.

"C'mon, Viv. Why don't you just spend some of it?" Addy demanded.

"You know that **charity** that helped William when he was sick?" Vivian said slowly. "Maybe they could really use it."

"But so could you! You worked hard to earn this." Addy waved a twenty-dollar bill. "Besides, you need to save money for college," she argued.

continued on next page

mount *v.*, get bigger
accessories *n.*, decorations, such as belts, hats, or purses
charity *n.*, organization that helps people

Monitor Your Reading

4. What ideas or vocabulary did you stop to clear up?

____

____

____

5. How did you clear up the confusion?

____

____

____

6. What do you predict Vivian will do with the money?

____

____

____

Plan and Monitor Your Reading, continued

A Key Decision, continued

"You don't understand what this means to me, do you?" she mused. "You don't have the faintest idea how little I care about the money."

Vivian chose a key ring and held it to the light. She rubbed the green and blue zigzag pattern between her fingers. The **texture** of the fabric was rough, but comforting.

She remembered when she made this one. It had been a rainy Thursday afternoon. William had just come home from his last **chemotherapy** session. He had looked weak, yet he wore a faint smile of victory. William was back in school now.

Vivian wondered how the other students had reacted to William's return. She could imagine them cheering and clapping for him. If only his full **recovery** could go as smoothly. There must be other students at the same school with physical problems. Across the country there must be thousands.

Vivian turned to Addy with a fiery gleam in her eyes. It was a look Addy knew all too well.

continued on next page

---

texture *n.*, how something feels when touched
chemotherapy *n.*, chemicals used to treat or control a disease
recovery *n.*, getting well

Check Your Understanding

7. What problem or conflict do the characters face?

Monitor Your Reading

8. Who have you known that Vivian or Addy reminds you of? Explain.

Plan and Monitor Your Reading, continued

A Key Decision, continued

"Give me that twenty, Addy. Most of this money can go to the charity," Vivian said. "And the rest will go to supplies. I just got a fabulous new idea for a hot seller!"

Addy smiled as she listened to Vivian's new dream. She admired her friend's talent and **drive**; she always had. Now she found herself admiring Vivian's big heart too. A saying popped into her head, "What goes around, comes around." Maybe she should just back off her **insistence** that Viv keep money for herself. All this charity work would certainly look good on Viv's college applications.

"Okay, Boss," Addy laughed. "Just tell me what to buy and how much of it. Let's get started."

---

drive *n.*, determination, energy
insistence *n.*, trying to convince

Sum It Up

9. In the story, what did Addy learn?

____

____

____

Monitor Your Reading

10. What connections did you make between the story and your own life?

____

____

____

____

Self-Assessment

11. How did planning and monitoring help you understand the story?

____

____

____

Name ______________________ Date __________

Plan and Monitor Your Reading

Before you begin to read, preview the text to get ready for what lies ahead. Preview "Fighting for the Right to Vote" and answer these questions.

Strategy at a Glance

Plan and Monitor Your Reading

When you plan and monitor your reading, you

- preview, make predictions, and think about your purpose
- check in with yourself to clear up confusing ideas and vocabulary.

1. What are the topic and genre of this selection?

   Topic: ______________________

   Genre: ______________________

2. What new information do you think you will learn about the topic from reading the selection?

   ____

   ____

Now read the selection. As you read, stay in control to get the most out of your reading.

DID YOU KNOW?

- Women in the U.S. gained the right to vote in 1920.
- Frederick Douglass was an escaped slave who worked for civil rights between 1841 and 1895.

Fighting for the Right to Vote

Leading the Way

It was 1872, and change was brewing in the United States. New laws in some states granted women the right to own property. A few universities began accepting female students. But one maverick wanted more. At a time when women did not even have the right to vote, Victoria Woodhull set her sights on the highest office of all. She wanted to be President.

Victoria Woodhull was born on September 23, 1838, in Ohio. During her childhood, Woodhull shocked **contemporary** society by cutting her hair short and choosing to wear men's clothing.

continued on next page

Victoria Woodhull

contemporary *adj.*, of the time

Plan and Monitor Your Reading, continued

Fighting for the Right to Vote, continued

Finding Her Voice

As she grew older, Woodhull found other ways to express her beliefs. In New York, she and her sister published *Woodhull and Claflin's Weekly,* which ran from 1870–1876. This paper featured **radical** articles about women's rights. Among other ideas, the paper **advocated** a woman's right to vote and wear short skirts. Woodhull believed that "women are the equals of men before the law, and are equal in all their rights."

Woodhull took this message all the way to Washington. In a **dynamic** speech, she declared that the Congressmen had misread the Constitution and that women already had the right to vote. However, she failed to convince them.

continued on next page

radical *adj.,* extreme
advocated *v.,* argued for
dynamic *adj.,* exciting

Monitor Your Reading

3. What ideas or vocabulary did you stop to clear up?

4. How did you clear up the confusion?

Check Your Understanding

5. What did Woodhull try to accomplish in her paper and speeches?

Plan and Monitor Your Reading, continued

Fighting for the Right to Vote, continued

Woodhull pressed on. She attempted to cast a ballot by bringing her key piece of evidence, a copy of the Constitution, to a polling station. Many of her fellow **suffragists** cheered her actions. Other suffragists thought Woodhull was too **controversial**. She upset some women's rights activists by claiming that the spirit of an ancient Greek **orator** named Demosthenes guided her decisions. Demosthenes lived in the fourth century in Athens, and Woodhull's claim was too fantastic for her time.

Ahead of Her Time

Despite her controversial reputation, many admired Woodhull. She was one of the most famous women in the U.S. and many considered her ahead of her time. Mostly, however, she was her own person. Although she was opposed to organized Christian religion, she lived its principles. She welcomed royalty and criminals alike into her home. She cared for the sick and visited prisoners.

continued on next page

Suffragists at the Ohio Statehouse

suffragists *n.,* believers in giving women the right to vote
controversial *adj.,* disagreeable or causing argument
orator *n.,* public speaker

Monitor Your Reading

6. What does Woodhull's story remind you of in your own life? Explain.

7. Describe a picture you had in your mind as you read the selection.

Plan and Monitor Your Reading, continued

Fighting for the Right to Vote, continued

Presidential Nominee

Ignoring her critics, Woodhull ran for President in 1872. She was nominated for President by the Equal Rights Party. The members of the Equal Rights Party were a very diverse group. They were laborers, suffragists, spiritualists, communists, and others. The one thing they agreed on was that the government needed reform.

Woodhull's running mate was Frederick Douglass. As an African American man, Douglass had recently been granted the right to vote. Voters had elected African American men to Congress and state legislatures. In Woodhull's opinion, it was time these doors were open to women, as well.

Although she lost her bid for the Presidency, Woodhull's influence extended far beyond her lifespan. Thanks in part to her work, today all women in the U.S. can vote.

Victoria Woodhull attempting to vote

Sum It Up

8. What will you remember most about Victoria Woodhull?

Monitor Your Reading

9. What connections did you make between the story and your own life?

Self-Assessment

10. How did planning and monitoring help you understand the selection?

Name ______________________ Date __________

Identify the Stated Main Idea

Preview "Avalanche Dogs to the Rescue" so that you know what to expect when you read. Then read the paragraph and underline the stated main idea.

Strategy at a Glance

Determine Importance

When you identify the stated main idea, you

- find the sentence that states what the writer is mostly saying about the topic
- check to see that the details support the main idea.

DID YOU KNOW?

- Snow can bury people and cut off air very quickly.
- Most avalanche victims survive if found within 15 minutes.

Avalanche Dogs to the Rescue

Was that a dog jumping off that ski lift chair? There he is, at the summit, barking and rolling in the snow. It's a dog all right, but don't be fooled. Harlan is not there to play. Harlan is a search and rescue (SAR) dog. Like all SAR dogs, Harlan's been training to save lives since he was a puppy. When a victim is buried in an avalanche, an SAR dog outworks 20 human rescuers. Sniffing madly, an SAR dog like Harlan can **detect** a person buried in up to 15 feet of **suffocating** snow. Search and rescue dogs have saved hundreds of lives worldwide.

Avalanche search and rescue dogs save lives.

detect *v.*, sense; find

suffocating *adj.*, making it impossible for people to breathe

Now show your thinking. Use the graphic organizer to map the main idea and details.

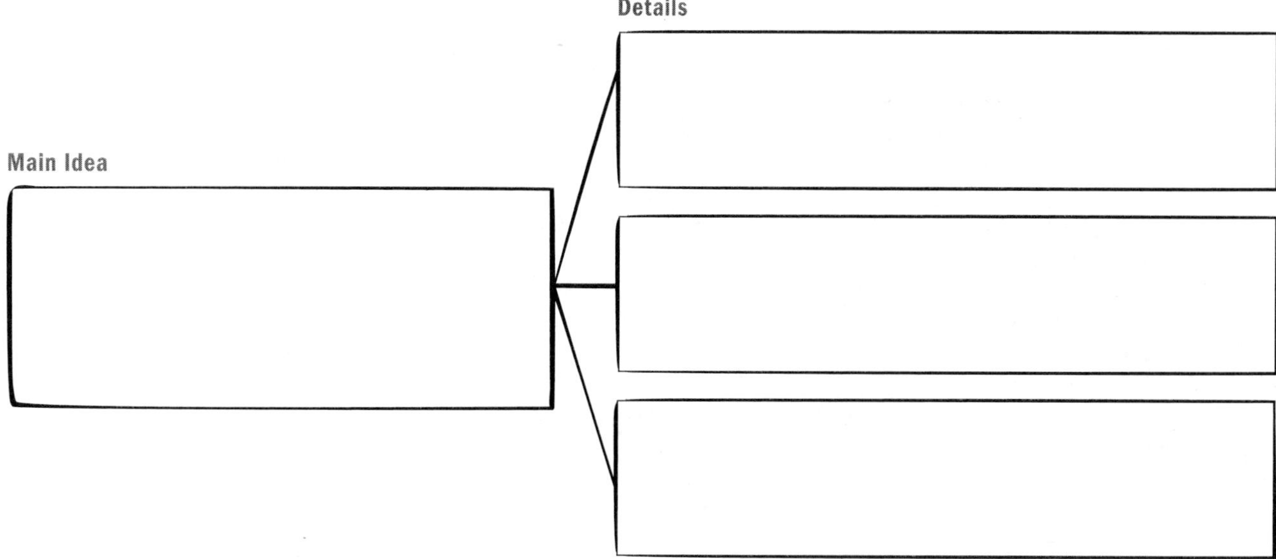

Preview "Digging to Survive" so that you know what to expect when you read. Then read the paragraph and underline the stated main idea.

DID YOU KNOW?

- Mount Hood in Oregon is more than 11,000 feet high.
- A snowstorm can develop quickly on such a high mountain.

Digging to Survive

Extreme winter storms threaten mountain hikers. Some hikers have proved that the best place to get warm in a raging snowstorm is in the snow itself. In 1976, three Oregon teenagers survived a snowstorm on Mount Hood. They knew that, in a snow cave, the snow **insulates** against the cold. The teens dug an entrance at the bottom of a **snowdrift**. Then they dug up towards the center of the drift. They poked a hole in the ceiling of their cave for fresh air and blocked in their entrance. The teens survived thirteen days until rescuers arrived.

Snow caves provide shelter from extreme winter weather.

insulates *v.*, keeps people warm
snowdrift *n.*, mound of snow created by wind

Use the graphic organizer to map the main idea and details.

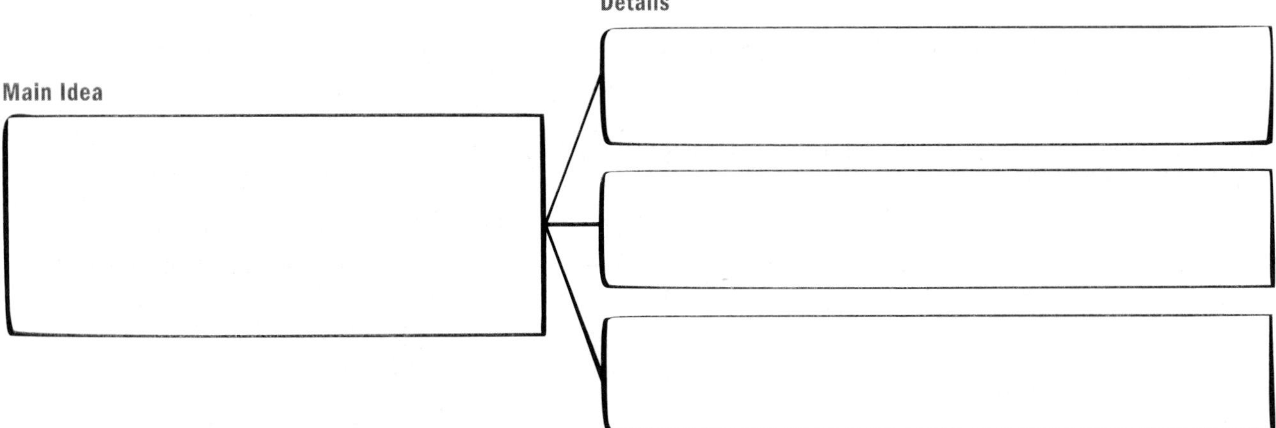

Talk About It
Compare your diagrams to a classmate's.

Make the Ideas Your Own
What did you know about surviving in a snow emergency before you read? What do you know about the topic now?

Name ____________________ Date __________

What If the Main Idea Isn't Stated?

Preview "Pride in the Sky" so that you know what to expect when you read. Then read the paragraph. Add up the details to figure out the main idea.

Strategy at a Glance

Determine Importance

When you infer the main idea, you

- look for clues to the topic, or what the selection is mostly about
- focus on important details
- combine details with what you know.

DID YOU KNOW?

- Mohawks are a Native American people of the Northeastern U.S.
- On 9/11/01, terrorists destroyed the World Trade Center in New York City.

The topic is

____

The important details are

+

What I already knew about the topic:

____

____

____

The details add up to:

____

____

____

Pride in the Sky

Ironworkers on a skyscraper in New York

"A lot of people think Mohawks aren't afraid of heights. That's not true. We have as much fear as the next guy. The difference is that we deal with it better," said Kyle, a Mohawk ironworker. For more than 100 years, Mohawk people have helped build New York City skyscrapers, including the Empire State Building in the 1930s. More **recently**, Mohawk workers helped build the World Trade Center and then clean up the site after the 9/11 disaster. Many people call them "Fearless Wonders." Mohawk ironworkers ignore the fact that they are walking on narrow strips of steel several hundred feet above the ground. They look as relaxed as if they were on a stroll through a forest path. Their **achievements** are a source of honor to the Mohawk people. As Kyle puts it, "There's pride in 'walking iron'."

recently *adv.*, not long ago
achievements *n.*, things people succeed in doing with effort

Preview "Medics and Pilots Save Lives" so that you know what to expect when you read. Then read the paragraph. Add up the details to figure out the main idea.

DID YOU KNOW?

- The Democratic Republic of Congo is in Africa.
- Measles can be deadly, especially in areas without modern medical care.

The topic is

____

The important details are

+

What I already knew about the topic:

____

____

____

____

Medics and Pilots Save Lives

Bush pilot in a remote area

Jessica Nestrell is a nurse. In 2004, she was working in the Democratic Republic of Congo. She knew that a measles epidemic would be especially challenging there. Diseases spread quickly in steamy rainforests. Nestrell knew that vaccines would prevent the disease. She also knew it would take a lot of teamwork to get the medicine to the villagers. First, a bush pilot had to **pinpoint** the villages. He risked his life landing in these **remote** areas. Then Nestrell and her team took the medicine by canoe through the rainforest. They risked their lives to keep the vaccines cool and prevent an epidemic.

pinpoint *v.,* locate
remote *adj.,* far away and hard to reach

The details add up to:

____

____

Talk About It

Tell your teacher or a classmate what you learned about the topic.

Name ____________________ Date __________

Summarize a Nonfiction Paragraph

Preview "Chasing Tornadoes" so that you know what to expect when you read. Then read the paragraph.

Strategy at a Glance

Determine Importance

When you summarize a nonfiction paragraph, you

- identify the topic
- find the main idea that most of the details tell about
- put the topic, main idea, and important details in your own words.

DID YOU KNOW?

- Tornadoes often are shaped like a funnel—narrow at the bottom and wide at the top.

Chasing Tornadoes

Tornado chasers love to pursue extreme weather. Their goal is to get close enough to tornadoes to measure and photograph them. They don't want to get hurt, however. How close is too close? Tornado chaser Tim Baker got one answer on June 9, 2003. During the chase, a hailstorm **erupted**. Then winds picked up a trailer. A board even crashed into his car! No one can predict a tornado's path. But whenever a storm spins into a funnel shape, know that a chaser is racing to catch up with it.

Tornado chasers watch violent storms up close.

erupted *v.*, began suddenly

Summarize the paragraph by identifying the topic, main idea, and details.

The Topic: ____________________

Main Idea

Details

My Summary: ____________________

Preview "Working Under Pressure" so that you know what to expect when you read. Then read the paragraph.

DID YOU KNOW?

- Commercial divers get special training.
- Divers work in many kinds of underwater conditions.

Working Under Pressure

It's the start of another workday. A **commercial** diver puts on a wetsuit, lugs equipment, and dives hundreds of feet down. These workers use their skills in extreme underwater environments to repair, build, or inspect equipment. They might be underwater plumbers. They might repair oilrigs. They all face danger. These divers use heavy tools that could break their air hoses. Sharks circle in the dark water. Then, divers have to swim back up carefully, or they might experience pain and even death from the **bends**. Experienced commercial divers can earn more than $100,000 per year. For them, surviving the risks might be as rewarding as the money.

Commercial divers work under water in dangerous conditions.

commercial *adj.,* receiving money for work done; professional
bends *n.,* painful sickness caused when divers come to the surface too quickly

Summarize the paragraph by identifying the topic, main idea, and details.

The Topic: ____________________

Main Idea

Details

My Summary: ____________________

Name ______________________ Date ____________

Summarize a Nonfiction Article

Preview "Surfers' Super Bowl" so that you know what to expect when you read. Then read and summarize the entire article.

Strategy at a Glance

Determine Importance

When you summarize a nonfiction article, you

- identify the topic
- notice ideas the writer emphasizes
- sum up the most important ideas and information in a brief statement.

DID YOU KNOW?

- Wind and coastal landforms create waves.
- Surfers ride the waves on special boards.

The Topic:

____

____

Some important details and information are

+

+

Surfers' Super Bowl

A monster wave at the Mavericks

The Call

Each winter, the world's best surfers pack their bags. Then they wait for a telephone call. When the call comes, they head to the San Mateo coast in northern California. The Mavericks Surf Contest is held there every year. However, nobody knows exactly when it will take place. The extreme weather that causes the monster waves is too **unpredictable**.

From January through March, large storms gain strength in the Pacific Ocean. These weather systems push giant waves toward the shore. Just before they reach the Mavericks, the waves pass through an underwater **trench**. Then the waves come out of the trench. They often explode with great force against the shallow **reef**. The result is some of the wildest waves anywhere in the world.

continued on next page

unpredictable *adj.*, cannot be predicted beforehand
trench *n.*, a long, narrow opening in the ocean floor
reef *n.*, a chain of rocks located near the surface of the sea

Some other important details and information are

+

My Summary:

____

____

____

____

____

____

____

____

____

____

____

____

____

____

____

____

Surfers' Super Bowl, continued

2006 Mavericks winner Grant "Twiggy" Baker

Those waves inspired the world's most unique surfing contest. The event is called the Mavericks Surf Contest. The event's organizers decide when the waves are powerful enough for this extreme sport. They also select and call the participants. Then the surfers have 24 hours to get to the Mavericks. Finally, the event begins.

The Danger

What else makes the waves at the Mavericks some of the most **treacherous** in the world? The waves crash into the jagged rocks of a reef. Unless surfers know how to avoid these rocks, they could be seriously injured. Great white sharks live in the waters. Yet only one shark attack has been recorded since people began surfing in the area.

The Appeal

Danger seems to **appeal to** the surfers in this contest. They dream of challenging nature at one of its wildest moments. Only the finest surfers in the world compete in "The Super Bowl of big-wave surfing." Those that are skillful enough to win can boast they have beaten the best at their game.

---

treacherous *adj.,* very dangerous
appeal to *v.,* attract

Name ______________________ Date ____________

Summarize Poetry

Preview the "The Winds of the World" so that you know what to expect when you read. Then read the poem.

Strategy at a Glance

Determine Importance

When you summarize poetry, you

- focus on what the poet is describing
- notice words that appeal to your senses
- tell the poet's message in your own words.

DID YOU KNOW?

- Writers often use the wind as a symbol of power.
- "The winds of war" and "the winds of change" are common expressions.

THE WINDS OF THE WORLD

—Rachel Bradford

Face to the spray, inhaling the **brutal** sea,
each gasp a sting of salt,
each gust a cracking whip—

I open my arms to the world's wind
holding fast against its snaps and shivers
pulsing with the raging storm.

Above, gulls fly in **feverish** flight
a ragged arc against the wind.
Do they hear only their dull wings' beat?

Do they leave to me the roar below?
I do not flee. I stay on this **promontory,**
welcoming the thundering waves that
break and break and break
in frothy **fury.**

---

brutal *adj.,* violent, forceful
feverish *adj.,* excited, restless
promontory *n.,* high peak of land
fury *n.,* passionate anger

Now summarize the poem to state the poet's message.

1. What is the poet describing?

____

2. Use a chart to record words that appeal to your senses and how they make you feel.

Lines from the Poem	How I Feel

The poet's message is ____

____

____

____

____

Talk About It

With your teacher or classmates, explore meanings you find in the poem. Point out lines in the poem that sparked your ideas.

Write About It

Explain how lines and words in the poem connect to the poet's message.

____

____

____

____

____

____

____

Name ______________________ Date ____________

Summarize Fiction

Preview "How First Man Escaped the Underworld" so that you know what to expect when you read. Then read the myth.

Strategy at a Glance

Determine Importance

When you summarize fiction, you

- identify the characters and setting
- focus on the conflict, or struggle the main character faces
- track the events of the story
- identify the resolution, or how the conflict ends.

DID YOU KNOW?

- Almost all cultures have creation myths.
- Some Native American children play a hide-and-seek game with a hidden object.

How First Man Escaped the Underworld

"Stop!" First Man shouted as he ran through the inky blackness of the Underworld. "You must listen to my idea!"

Owl laughed and **taunted** First Man, soaring far above him.

First Man dreamed that daytime would rule the Underworld. Owl loved only the dark, so the arguing did not cease.

"My idea is a game. If you win the game, nighttime will rule the Underworld. But if you lose, light will enter the Underworld."

After some thought, Owl agreed. First Man gave Badger a small white disc to hide deep in the forest. The two competitors agreed to cover their eyes with a cup made of thin wood and race to find the disc.

Owl's excellent eyesight made him confident. But the cup did not fit over his eyes easily. And how different the Underworld looked through the tiny slits in the bark! Owl struggled as he searched. Meanwhile, First Man was relying on his hands and feet more than his eyesight. Owl did not know that First Man had practiced the game and learned this **advantage.**

Around them, the creatures who dreamed First Man's dream hoped for light. The creatures who loved nighttime cheered for Owl. After many hours, First Man's fingers touched a smooth, round object. "Now we shall meet the sun!" he cried.

At that very moment, light flooded the Underworld. Owl hooted and shrieked, as he covered his eyes with his wings. The other creatures stared in wonder as the rays revealed an opening to Earth. Finally, they would be able to leave the Underworld.

---

taunted *v.*, mocked

advantage *n.*, something that helps someone do something

Focus on the main characters, setting, and events to summarize the myth.

1. Who are the main characters?

____

2. What is the setting?

____

3. Complete the story map to track what happens.

Story Map

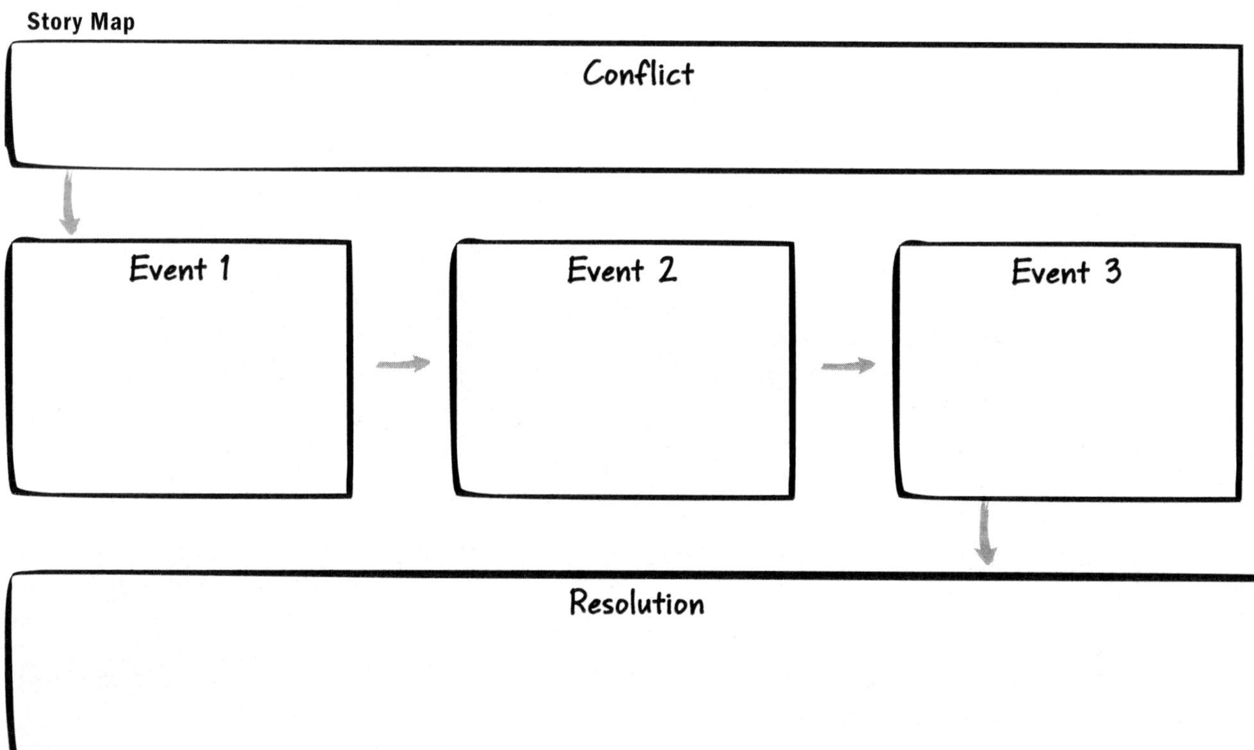

Talk About It

Tell your teacher or a classmate a summary of the myth.

Make the Ideas Your Own

Compare this myth to other myths you know. How are they alike? How are they different?

____

____

____

____

____

Name ________________________________ Date ______________

Focus on Your Purpose

Preview "Diving in Extreme Environments." What is the topic?

Topic: ________________________________

Now use this chart to help you set a purpose. Fill in the first two columns.

Strategy at a Glance

Determine Importance

To read with a purpose, you

- think about what you already know about the topic
- decide what you want to learn
- develop a list of questions and answer them as you read.

What I KNOW	What I WANT TO KNOW	What I LEARNED

Read the purpose and focus on your purpose. Then complete the third column of the chart.

DID YOU KNOW?

- Diving can be as dangerous as skydiving.
- Different kinds of diving require different equipment.

Diving in Extreme Environments

Free Diving

Mehgan Heaney-Grier sits on the beach. She slips on her long, flexible scuba fins. Next, she puts on her soft mask and a simple snorkel. Then she slides into the water.

She **treads water** for a few minutes and breathes slowly and deeply. Her heart rate drops to fifty-five beats per minute. She takes a full breath and **jackknifes** to point her head downward. In twenty seconds, she **descends** to about fifty feet underwater.

Without belts, tanks, or other gear, Mehgan glides along like a fish. She gazes at the gorgeous sights. She gives a few kicks and heads for the surface. She exhales hard and inhales. That first taste of air is wonderful!

Free divers use simple equipment.

continued on next page

treads water *v.*, moves one's arms and legs to stay above the water
jackknifes *v.*, changes direction sharply
descends *v.*, moves downward

Preview the second part of the article and identify the topic. Use the chart to help you set a purpose. Fill in the first two columns.

Topic: ______________________________

What I KNOW	What I WANT TO KNOW	What I LEARNED

Read the second part of the article and focus on your purpose. Then complete the third column of the chart.

Diving in Extreme Environments, continued

Cave Diving

Michael O'Leary turns through tunnels under water. He marvels at an environment few people will ever see. It is Jackson Blue Cave, west of Tallahassee, Florida. The group Michael takes through the cave is lucky. They are among the one percent of divers skilled enough to become cave divers. Michael has **tallied** over one thousand dives like this one.

Now the divers are far beyond the reach of sunlight. Each diver uses one light and carries two backups. Michael checks his air supply. He has only used one third, but turns back. The group follows a rope that clearly marks their path. Why all the **precautions**? Michael never wants to be caught in this underwater maze without the skills and supplies to make it out alive.

Michael and the divers hover in the cavern. They are waiting for their bodies to adjust. Then they move upward slowly to avoid getting the bends. Michael makes sure he can add another safe dive to his record.

Cave divers use special equipment.

---

tallied *v.*, completed
precautions *n.*, safety measures

Talk About It

Tell your teacher or a classmate what you learned about free diving and cave diving. Did you find answers to all your questions? If not, tell what you can do to find the answers.

Name ______________________ Date ____________

What Speaks to You?

Preview "Pole Explorers" so that you know what to expect when you read. As you read the text, connect with what's important to you.

Strategy at a Glance

Determine Importance

To find ideas that speak to you, think about

- the topic and what you know about it
- the writer's opinions or descriptions
- what seems worth remembering or sharing.

DID YOU KNOW?

- Robert Peary and Matthew Henson explored the North Pole.
- Native people, called the Inuit, helped the explorers.

The topic is

____

____

____

1. What do you already know about the topic?

____

____

____

____

____

2. Which ideas or information stand out?

____

____

____

____

____

____

____

____

____

____

____

Pole Explorers

Henson was one of the first to reach the North Pole.

On April 5, Peary checked the position of the sun with his **sextant**. It told him that the Pole was only 35 miles away. The next morning, he alerted Henson. It was time to begin the march. Henson set out with his Inuit companions. Their progress was very successful. They covered 20 miles. By that time Henson was an hour ahead of Peary.

Then Henson had to drive his team across thin ice. The ice suddenly cracked. Henson, along with his dogs and **sledge**, plunged into the icy water. Henson began floundering about. He tried to grasp onto jutting ice to save himself. He swallowed **frigid** water. His lungs felt like they would burst. Then he found himself being lifted out of the water. It was Ootah who saved him. Ootah saved his sledge and the dogs, too. Ootah slipped off Henson's wet boots and warmed his feet in the Inuit way. He held Henson's feet against his bare stomach.

continued on next page

sextant *n.,* a tool used to determine geographical location
sledge *n.,* a type of wooden sled
frigid *adj.,* extremely cold

3. What do you think of the author's writing and ideas?

4. What seems worth remembering or sharing?

Talk About It

Tell your teacher or a classmate about the parts of the article that spoke to you.

Make the Ideas Your Own

What have you learned about North Pole explorers? How has the selection changed your thinking?

Pole Explorers, continued

Henson and four Inuit at the North Pole

Henson had learned to steer a ship by the stars. He had often played a game with Peary. He said that he could estimate their position at the end of each day's march. They continued marching for four more hours. Then Henson deduced that they must have reached the North Pole.

Henson, Ooqueah, and Ootah built igloos. Peary arrived forty-five minutes later. When the clouds parted in the sky, he took a reading with his sextant. The reading **affirmed** Henson's estimate. They were within five miles of the North Pole. The **expedition** had reached its goal. It was April 6, 1909. In a whisper, Peary announced his reading to Henson. Then the two weary explorers crawled into an igloo. They lay down and went to sleep.

When Peary awoke, he wrote in his diary, "The Pole at last!!!" Peary had carried a thin silk American flag during his many years of exploration. He carefully unpacked the precious flag. Then he planted it on top of his igloo.

affirmed *v.*, proved
expedition *n.*, journey made for a purpose

Name ______________________ Date ____________

Determine Importance

Preview "Extreme Pressure" so that you know what to expect when you read. As you read, focus on what's important. Mark the text and take notes.

Strategy at a Glance

Determine Importance

When you determine importance, you

- figure out the main idea
- summarize the main idea and important details
- look for what speaks to you.

DID YOU KNOW?

- Symptoms of claustrophobia may include sweating, shaking, and nausea.
- Cave explorers carry extra lights, batteries, and bulbs.

EXTREME PRESSURE

"Jasmine, you have to go first," Ms. Donnelly ordered.

"What!?" Jasmine was terrified to even step inside a cave, let alone enter a dark tunnel first.

"You crawl through first. If your **claustrophobia** stops you from going any further, then none of us will go. We're a team down here in this cave, and that means everywhere we go, we go together," said Ms. Donnelly.

Jasmine was the most athletic student in the group, but she was also claustrophobic. Could she **defeat** her fears while crawling on her belly through a two-foot high, very narrow, pitch-black tunnel?

continued on next page

claustrophobia *n.*, fear of enclosed spaces
defeat *v.*, conquer; overcome

Check Your Understanding

1. Identify the characters and setting of the story.

____

____

2. What conflict does Jasmine face?

____

____

Determine Importance, continued

Extreme Pressure, continued

"Jasmine, take a few deep breaths. Relax your body, lie on the ground, and focus on this task. Okay, get comfortable in the position. That's right. Take a few more breaths. Now just start **inching** forward. Remember it's not a race, and I know you can do this." Ms. Donnelly was an expert cave explorer. Her calm voice and simple instructions helped Jasmine focus.

Leading, the girl crept **tentatively** forward. Before she knew it, her body was halfway into the tunnel. Jasmine strained to see the end of the tunnel, but she could only see darkness. Her heart began to pound and her mind took off. She saw herself imprisoned in the tunnel and growing faint with hunger and thirst. Rescue workers would not reach her in time...

"Focus on the present moment," Jasmine reminded herself. "See only what is real right now."

Jasmine focused on the **abrasive** walls of the cave scratching her skin. She realized that she could move around a bit; she was not trapped. She heard the flapping of bats' wings, but none sounded close enough to touch her. The sound of slowly dripping water echoed throughout the cave, but her skin felt perfectly dry.

continued on next page

inching *v.,* moving slowly
tentatively *adv.,* carefully, with some hesitation
abrasive *adj.,* with a rough surface

Determine Importance

3. What does Ms. Donnelly do? Why are these actions important?

4. What does Jasmine do? Why are these actions important?

Determine Importance, continued

Extreme Pressure, continued

Continuing to focus on her physical surroundings, Jasmine began to move forward again. Soon she became aware of the sound of thunder sweeping toward her. The noise seemed to **originate** ahead of her and soon filled the tunnel with a constant roar. Jasmine gasped as her panic began to build.

"What—what's that?" she yelled. She was sure rocks were loosening and the tunnel was about to collapse on her.

"That's the waterfall! You're almost there, Jasmine!" Ms. Donnelly's clear voice came forward like a light piercing the inky tunnel, and Jasmine could sense that the end of the tunnel was near.

The ceiling of the tunnel seemed to rise slightly. Jasmine found that she could now lift her chest and belly off the floor of the tunnel. She **maneuvered** her body until she was able to bend her knees. A small push forward and she was crawling!

"I never thought I'd find crawling exciting," she thought. "This experience has already changed my **perspective**."

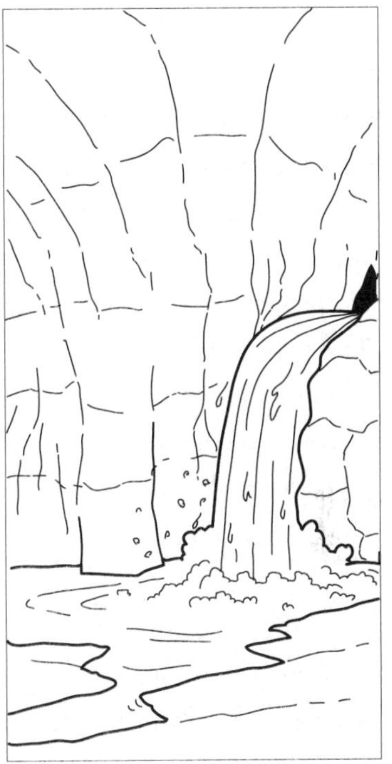

continued on next page

originate *v.,* come from
maneuvered *v.,* moved around obstacles
perspective *n.,* point of view; outlook on life

Check Your Understanding

5. How has Jasmine's thinking changed?

Determine Importance

6. Summarize the events that have happened so far.

Determine Importance, continued

Extreme Pressure, continued

A rush of damp, cool air bathed Jasmine's hot face. She looked to her left and found that the light from her headlamp traveled several feet before hitting glistening **stalactites** dripping water onto the **stalagmites** below. She turned to the right and her light revealed only open space. Finally, she gazed ahead. Her light traveled far ahead of her before hitting the froth of the waterfall.

Jasmine was so amazed she jumped to her feet and then realized she could stand up!

"I made it!" she yelled. "That waterfall is the most beautiful sight I've ever seen! And the rest of the cave is gorgeous, too! Are all caves this amazing?"

"Pretty much," smiled Ms. Donnelly. "Want to see what lies ahead through the next tunnel?"

"Sure," Jasmine smiled at her classmates. "I'm an experienced **spelunker** now and my claustrophobia seems to have disappeared. Does someone else want to go first this time?"

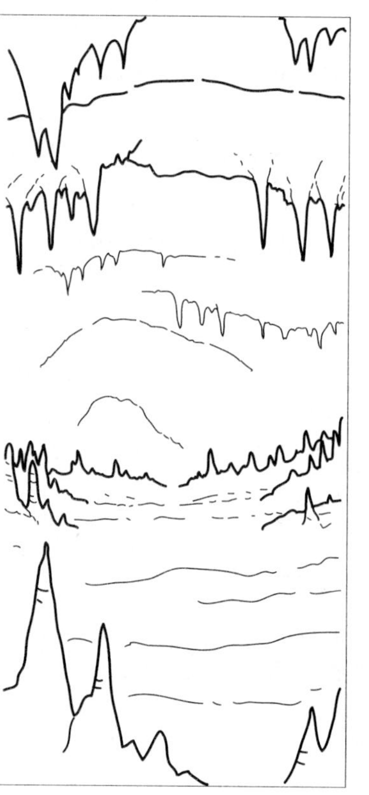

---

stalactites *n.*, stone formations that hang down from a cave's roof or sides
stalagmites *n.*, stone formations that rise up from a cave floor
spelunker *n.*, cave explorer

Determine Importance

7. Summarize "Extreme Pressure."

8. What ideas in the story were important to you? Explain why.

Self-Assessment

9. How did focusing on what is important help you understand the story?

Determine Importance

Preview "Big Wall Climbing" so that you know what to expect when you read. Then answer the question.

1. List three questions that you expect the passage to answer.

____

____

____

____

Strategy at a Glance

Determine Importance

When you determine importance, you

- figure out the main idea
- summarize the main idea and important details
- look for what speaks to you.

Now read the selection. As you read, focus on what's important. Mark the text and take notes.

DID YOU KNOW?

- Big wall climbing is one type of rock climbing.
- El Capitan is a famous rock formation in Yosemite National Park in California.

Big Wall Climbing

Climbing El Capitan

El Capitan soars into the bright blue sky. Imagine El Capitan next to the Empire State Building. The cliff is more than twice as high as the skyscraper. This enormous rock cliff in California attracts big wall climbers from all over the world.

Today a team of climbers is halfway up the **sheer** face of this immense tower of stone. All the way up, the team battles wind and **fatigue**.

El Capitan towers above the valley floor.

continued on next page

sheer *adj.*, steep and flat
fatigue *n.*, being extremely tired

Check Your Understanding

2. What is El Capitan? Why is it difficult to climb?

____

____

Determine Importance, continued

Big Wall Climbing, continued

These extreme athletes haven't touched level ground for two days. Their hands and feet are swollen. Cuts and scrapes cover their bodies. Their shoulders ache from hauling huge bags of gear up **taut** ropes. After climbing all day, each climber unloads a portaledge. A portaledge is a portable tent system. The climber secures the portaledge to the cliff's steep face. Then each weary climber falls asleep, suspended in midair.

A climber asleep in a portaledge

Preparation and Practice

Climbers do not attempt **feats** like this without preparing. They undertake hours of training. They make many practice climbs before they qualify to take on El Capitan.

continued on next page

taut *adj.,* stretched tightly
feats *n.,* achievements

Check Your Understanding

3. What did you learn about big wall climbing?

4. Why do you think the climbers haven't been on level ground for two days?

5. Which details tell you that big wall climbing is dangerous?

Determine Importance, continued

Big Wall Climbing, continued

Big wall climbers also rely on specialized equipment. It takes a long time before they become experts. They must learn how to use the ropes, hooks, and metal spikes correctly. These tools allow them to make the big climbs safely.

Big wall climbers must carry daily survival equipment. They take high-energy food they need to maintain muscle power. They also pack water bottles, meals, a **portable** stove, and sleeping gear. Some of the bags weigh more than two hundred pounds.

Fitness and Endurance

Only special athletes can scale a raw rock face like El Capitan's. These athletes must have extraordinary skill and strength. Big wall climbers rely on natural **grooves** and cracks in the surface of the rock to move upward. They do all this while dangling hundreds or thousands of feet above the valley floor.

continued on next page

Scaling a sheer face

portable *adj.*, moveable and easy to carry
grooves *n.*, openings

Check Your Understanding

6. How do climbers prepare for a big wall climb?

Determine Importance

7. What is the main idea of the section "Fitness and Endurance"?

8. What ideas in the article are most important to you? Explain why.

Determine Importance, continued

Big Wall Climbing, continued

The Rewards

Although big wall climbing is **rigorous,** its rewards are great. Most climbers scarcely remember the pain they suffer as they ascend. Until they share stories after the climb, that is. Then they recount the terror and thrills. They share a sense of accomplishment at the end of a great climb.

Now, the **summit** is near, but it is dusk. The climbers set up portaledges. Then they dig out freeze-dried **rations** for dinner. As the sun sets, each climber savors an individual golden view. They fall asleep dreaming about the spectacular sights that await them at the top. Tomorrow, they will conquer El Capitan.

View from the top of El Capitan

---

rigorous *adj.,* difficult, requires great endurance
summit *n.,* top of a mountain
rations *n.,* food

Determine Importance

9. Summarize "Big Wall Climbing."

Self-Assessment

10. How did focusing on what is important help you understand the article?

Name ______________________ Date ____________

Fiction: Do You Get It?

As you read "Anansi Connects the World," ask and answer questions to make sure you understand the story.

Strategy at a Glance

Ask Questions

To make sure you understand fiction, you

- preview and ask questions before reading
- ask questions about characters, events, and words while reading
- ask big questions after reading.

DID YOU KNOW?

- Anansi is a character in African folktales.
- Folktales are traditional stories of a culture.
- Anansi is often a spider and sometimes walks like a man.

Write questions and answers.

1. My question before reading:

____

____

____

____

My answer:

____

____

____

____

2. My question about the characters and events:

____

____

____

____

My answer:

____

____

____

____

____

Anansi Connects the World

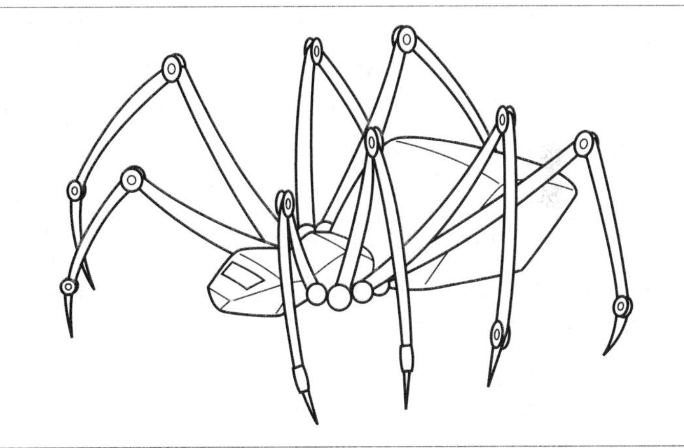

In this day and age, cell phones are in everyone's pockets. It was not always so! You can thank Anansi, the Robotic Spider, for your easy communication. Anansi was not really a hero, though. His greed, not cleverness, brought the cellular service you use every day.

The world was very new. The Sky King, Verbosus, wanted everyone to be able to **communicate** easily. He called Anansi. "A pox on drums, horns, and phone wires!" he declared. "Here!" To Anansi, he **entrusted** a metal briefcase. It held the entire cellular network. "You must create a communication network," he commanded. "Do it any way you can."

"Any way at all?" Anansi asked, with glittering eyes.

Verbosus mistook the greedy gleam in the spider's eyes for goodwill. "Do your best," he nodded.

continued on next page

---

communicate *v.*, talk

entrusted *v.*, gave something to another person for care

3. My question about what a word means:

____

____

My answer:

____

____

____

____

4. My Big Question after reading:

____

____

____

____

My answer:

____

____

____

____

Anansi Connects the World, continued

As the Sky King turned away, Anansi leaped with **glee.** All four pairs of mechanical feet clicked. Only those who would pay the highest premium would get cell phone service.

"But where can I hide this **priceless** case until then?" he wondered aloud.

Futuros, the Winds of Change, watched. "Anansi must never control this," they whispered.

Anansi gazed up at the tallest building in the United States. "Yes, it will be safe at the top of the Sears Tower," he decided. In the dead of night, Anansi crept to its base. He gripped the briefcase and began his climb. At about 100 yards, he fell.

"Uumph!" Anansi moaned. He picked himself up from the concrete. Then he started again, eager to gain his future power. The top was just a spider toe away. Then Futuros sent a 140-mile gust of wind. It whooshed over Anansi. The wind knocked Anansi into a free fall. Desperately, he caught a window ledge with one foot. The briefcase, however, slipped from his grasp.

Anansi watched the briefcase fall. It hit an **adjacent** building and burst open. Hundreds of **billowing** clouds floated out. Futuros pushed the clouds over the city and beyond. The communications network went everywhere. Now it gives the power of wireless phone service to all.

---

glee *n.,* great happiness
priceless *adj.,* very valuable
adjacent *adj.,* next to
billowing *adj.,* moving like a wave

Talk About It

Talk with your teacher or a classmate about questions you answered before, during, and after reading.

Make the Ideas Your Own

Retell the story to a classmate. What are the ideas you will remember? ______________________________

____

____

____

____

Name ______________________ Date __________

Nonfiction: Do You Get It?

As you read "Stepping into the Future," ask and answer questions to make sure you understand the article.

Strategy at a Glance

Ask Questions

To make sure you understand nonfiction, you

- preview and ask questions before reading
- ask questions about facts and ideas while reading
- ask questions to review after reading.

DID YOU KNOW?

- Many blind people use canes to find their way.
- People teach the blind how to use special technology.

Write questions and answers.

1. My question before reading:

____

____

____

____

My answer:

____

____

____

____

2. My question about facts and ideas:

____

____

____

____

My answer:

____

____

____

____

Stepping Into the Future

Today's Technology

"If I'm walking next to a wall or if I walk by a pole, the air will suddenly change. I can feel it on my skin." That's how Lucia Florez, who is blind, describes her ability to sense where things are. The blind, she says, are always thinking about moving around without bumping into things.

A teacher helps a blind person learn to use a cane.

Like most working adults, Florez uses computer programs. She can scan and read her snail mail. She can check her e-mail online. Her computer converts the on-screen display to speech. Yet, finding a classroom or a dentist office is difficult for her. To move about as freely as sighted people do, blind people have used a white cane or a guide dog. A cane can only touch a few feet ahead. What about objects that are farther away? A guide dog is well trained. Can something **communicate** better?

continued on next page

communicate *v.*, give information

3. Ask another question about facts and ideas:

My answer:

4. Ask another question about facts and ideas:

My answer:

Talk About It
Tell your teacher or a classmate what is important to remember about this article.

Make the Ideas Your Own
How do you depend on technology? How would your everyday life be different without technology?

Stepping Into the Future, continued

The Virtual Cane

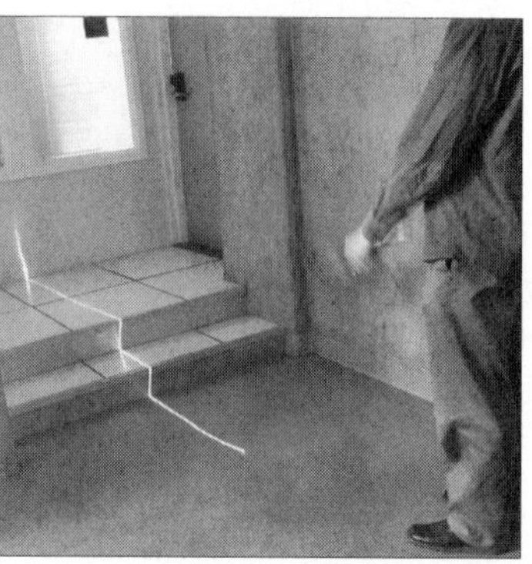
The laser device can detect objects.

Imagine that your vision is **impaired**. You are walking in a shopping mall. You take a slim **device** out of your pocket. You swing it before you from side to side as you walk and a red laser beam touches objects ahead. You hear sounds. They tell you a bench is ten feet away. You know a ramp is ahead, and slopes up at a 20-degree angle. You can't see all this. Yet you know every detail about what's around you.

UC Santa Cruz Professor Roberto Manduchi is working on a laser device that he believes will someday work as smoothly as that. It contains a camera to record the laser beams. It also has a computer to convert the data to useable information. But at this point the device is definitely not a fashion accessory. The bulky object looks like something out of a 1950s science fiction movie. The sounds are a problem, too. He admits that the constant high- and low-pitched beeping can be irritating.

The Future

Manduchi was encouraged when he tested and used the same technology on robots to help them **navigate**. The next tests will be with blind people. It will be tougher and longer. They will also be more costly. With funding from the National Science Foundation, Manduchi is continuing the testing.

impaired *adj.,* damaged or injured
device *n.,* machine or tool
navigate *v.,* move around

Name ______________________ Date __________

Question-Answer Relationships

Preview "Kyle's Gift" so that you know what to expect when you read. As you read the story, ask and answer questions. Tell where you found the answers.

Strategy at a Glance

Ask Questions

A good reader asks different types of questions while reading.

- For some questions, the answers are right there in the text.
- For some questions, you have to put together different parts of the text to find answers.

DID YOU KNOW?

- Some imagined "gifts" can have hidden dangers.
- An ancient story about King Midas tells how a gift became a disaster.

Write questions and answers.

1. My question before reading:

____

____

____

____

My answer:

____

____

____

____

I found the answer:

❑ one place in the text

❑ in different parts of the text

KYLE'S GIFT

Everything was different, starting tonight. Kyle would be alone forever, but no one could know the reason.

It had started at the homecoming dance when Kyle had picked up Laina and put on her wrist **corsage.** There in Laina's living room, Kyle saw the rest of the night. He saw Paul in his yellow polka-dotted vest arrive late to the dance. He saw James twist his ankle in the middle of his usual ridiculous dance moves. Future events popped into his head.

Kyle hadn't told anyone about his **foresight**. Every minute was too remarkable and astonishing to share. Then today, the dazzle had ended when he had handed a pen to Lynesha and felt an electric shock of horror. A car crash flashed before him. Helpless, he watched the **vision** continue. Lynesha was sobbing and bruised, but walking away.

All of these visions were disturbing. But what did they mean? Was Kyle just imagining these awful scenes? Or was he actually seeing the future? Time would tell.

continued on next page

---

corsage *n.*, flowers worn at a formal event
foresight *n.*, ability to see events before they happen
vision *n.*, mental image

2. My question during reading:

____

____

____

____

My answer:

____

____

____

____

I found the answer:

❑ one place in the text

❑ in different parts of the text

Talk About It

Talk to your teacher or a classmate about your questions and where you found answers.

Make the Ideas Your Own

What would it be like to see the future? Do you think it would be a good thing? Explain your answer.

Kyle's Gift, continued

When Kyle got home, his dad tried to greet him with a friendly punch on the arm, but Kyle swerved just in time and fled to his room. The thought of seeing his own father's future horrified him.

Downstairs his parents were talking.

"The doctor said it should start right around now," said his mother. "Should we tell him?"

"No, Ellen, the **treatment** may not have worked," his father replied. "I want Kyle to have this. I want him to have the power."

"Oh, this might be a terrible mistake. He's been so quiet lately." Ellen nervously twisted the napkin in her lap.

Kyle stood in the doorway to his room, **stunned**. "They did this to me," he whispered.

"Dinner, Son!" his father called.

"Why, Kyle!" said his mother brightly when he appeared with the hood of his sweatshirt pulled over his brow. "What's new?"

---

treatment *n.,* medical care
stunned *adj.,* shocked

____

____

____

____

____

____

____

____

____

____

Name ____________________ Date ____________

On Your Own Answers

Preview "UFO Attack" so that you know what to expect when you read. As you read, ask and answer questions about how the information fits with what you know.

Strategy at a Glance

Ask Questions

A good reader asks different types of questions while reading.

- Sometimes you need to use your own ideas and experiences to answer questions.

Write questions and answers.

1. My question:

   My answer:

   This fits with what I know because ____________________

2. My question:

   My answer:

   This fits with what I know because ____________________

UFO Attack

DAY 1: I feel **compelled** to keep this journal for any of my species who come after me, if any humans will. My air supply is limited, so I write **succinctly**, keeping my breathing relaxed and slow.

DAY 2: First the spaceships descended on the center of our city, skyscrapers crumbled from the vibrations, and many **succumbed** in that fashion. Then came the death-rays.

DAY 3: The death-rays seemed able to penetrate all protective devices so that those who survived did so by burrowing deep underground and sheltering there. Weakness comes upon me quickly now...

DAY 4: I had contact with another human. She has survived in a school basement. She has a radio and two days of food and water left. I told her to be strong.

DAY 5: Save yourselves, my fellow humans! Burrow into Mother Earth and let her protect you. I can write no more...

compelled *v.*, forced
succinctly *adv.*, briefly
succumbed *v.*, died

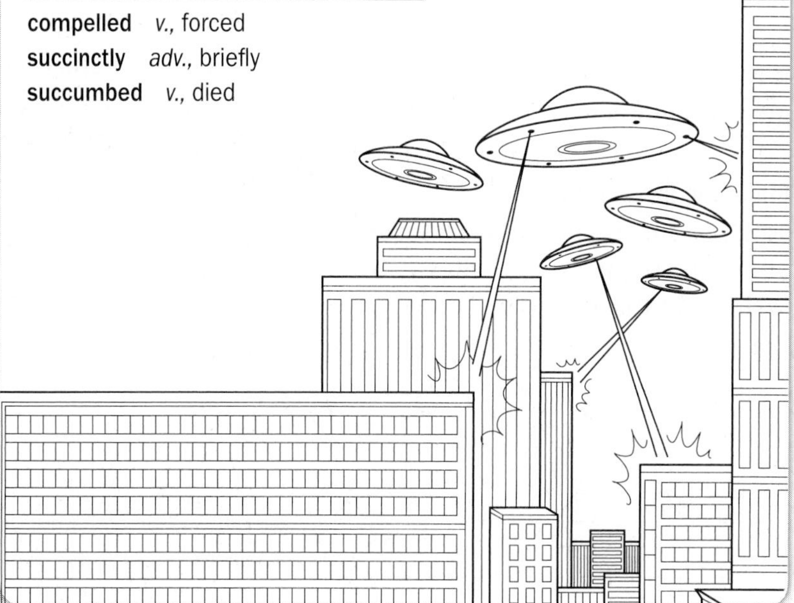

Preview "Killer Asteroid Defense" so that you know what to expect when you read. As you read, ask and answer questions about how the information fits with what you know.

DID YOU KNOW?

- Asteroids are rocks that fly around in space.
- Most asteroids orbit between Jupiter and Mars.

3. My question:

____

____

____

My answer:

____

____

____

This fits with what I know because _______________

____

____

____

Talk About It

Tell a classmate what new information you learned and how it fit with what you already knew about the topic.

Make the Ideas Your Own

Talk to your teacher or a classmate about the big ideas in the text. Write your discussion questions below.

____

____

____

____

Killer Asteroid Defense

Crater in Arizona caused by an asteroid

Imagine a giant asteroid zooming straight toward Earth. If it hits, disaster strikes! Tidal waves and earthquakes could result. Some asteroids may measure nearly 600 miles across. If one of those hits Earth, entire continents could disappear.

If an asteroid's **orbit** happens to cross a planet's orbit, the two may **collide**. Astronomer Duncan Steel says that this will happen to Earth someday. Disaster will strike unless we find a way to stop it.

Are we prepared to defend ourselves against a killer asteroid? Scientists are working on that very question. We already can determine when an asteroid is on a crash course with Earth. We just need to do something about it. Scientists want to create a global search and tracking shield. It would be expensive. But any expense is worth saving the world from catastrophe.

orbit *n.*, curved path around an object in space
collide *v.*, crash into each other

Name ____________________ Date ____________

Author & You Answers

Preview "The Future of Food" so that you know what to expect when you read. As you read, ask and answer questions to help you get inside the writer's head.

Strategy at a Glance

Ask Questions

To get inside the writer's head, you ask questions about

- why the author wrote the passage
- whether the text includes facts, opinions, or both.

DID YOU KNOW?

- Genes contain DNA.
- Scientists can change genes to produce a specific plant or animal.

Write questions and answers.

1. My question about the author's purpose:

____

____

____

____

My answer and how I know:

____

____

____

____

2. List one fact the writer presents and one opinion.

Fact: ____________________

____

____

____

Opinion: ____________________

____

____

____

____

____

The Future of Food

Purple carrots may appear in your school's cafeteria one day. If they do, it's probably an **engineered** food. The genes in the purple carrots have been changed.

A carrot with modified genes

Why are scientists modifying plants? The six billion people on our planet need a lot of food. Engineered foods can be easier to grow and produce more. Scientists hope that these plants will have more nutrients and taste better.

What's the catch? Some people object to genetically modified foods. They believe that such foods hold hidden threats. They might harm the environment and people's health. People are concerned that the plants could cause allergies. They think the foods might make us **resistant** to medications.

No one knows the actual effects that engineered plants will have on other **organisms**. But it's clear that we need food solutions. With the right controls, engineered foods might help.

---

engineered *v.*, changed from its natural state
resistant *adj.*, unable to benefit from
organisms *n.*, living things

Preview "Erica Discovers Cake." As you read, ask and answer questions.

DID YOU KNOW?

- Today many people's diets lack basic nutrients.
- Many people today take pills to replace nutrients missing from their diets.

3. My question about the author's purpose:

____

____

____

My answer and how I know:

____

____

____

____

Talk About It

Talk to your teacher or a classmate about the two passages and whether or not the writers achieved their purposes.

Make the Ideas Your Own

What did you learn about people's attitude toward food from reading the two passages?

____

____

____

____

____

____

____

____

____

Erica Discovers Cake

"GGG has amazing ancient books," thought Erica, as she stared at shelves reaching to the ceiling. Her great-great-grandfather loved to collect historical things like books.

"**Uploading** the information into your mind is quick, but where's the fun?" GGG always asked. At the age of 136 years, GGG still read books page-by-page.

Erica steered her **hovercraft** to a shelf labeled "History of Food." She grabbed *Food in the 21st Century.* She skipped over pictures of meat and bread and flipped to the "Desserts" section. It read: *The dessert ritual involved eating sweets at the end of a meal.* This was perfect for her history project!

Erica couldn't tear her eyes away from the cake. Suddenly, she felt her mouth watering. She had heard that this happened back when people used to eat food. Pills had replaced food before Erica was born. With meal pills no one went hungry. And no one gained weight. But Erica craved cake!

Erica parked the hovercraft and went to look for GGG. If anyone could help her make a cake, he could!

---

uploading *v.,* to move information
hovercraft *n.,* imaginary small airplane

Name ______________________ Date __________

Author & You Answers

Preview "Filmmakers' Visions" so that you know what to expect when you read. As you read, ask and answer questions to help you understand the writer's point of view.

Strategy at a Glance

Ask Questions

To understand the writer's point of view, you ask

- if the author has a personal connection with the topic
- why the author chose certain words.

DID YOU KNOW?

- Science fiction filmmakers base their films on science and add made-up ideas of their own.
- Special effects make all the events seem real.

Write questions and answers.

1. My question about the author's point of view:

____

____

____

____

____

My answer and how I know: (List words and phrases that reveal the writer's point of view.)

____

____

____

____

____

____

____

____

____

____

____

____

____

Filmmakers' Visions

Star Trek's vision of a vehicle of the future

Some of your ideas of the future have come from actual space ship launchings and landings. Others have been shaped by talented filmmakers.

Star Trek

In 1966, Gene Roddenberry created *Star Trek*. This television series **influenced** how modern viewers see the future. Viewers experienced faster-than-light space travel. They also met a cast of fascinating characters.

Star Wars

George Lucas wrote and directed the six-film series *Star Wars*. Early **episodes** recount the journey of Anakin Skywalker, a slave boy. Later, the boy becomes Darth Vader. Vader is master of an evil empire. Lucas thrilled audiences with amazing special effects.

---

influenced *v.*, had an effect
episodes *n.*, parts of a story

Preview "The Field Trip" so that you know what to expect when you read. As you read, ask and answer questions to help you understand the writer's point of view.

DID YOU KNOW?

- A wormhole is an idea scientists have about how time might work in outer space.
- A wormhole may be a shortcut through space.

Write questions and answers.

2. My question about the author's point of view:

___

___

___

My answer and how I know: (List words and phrases that reveal the writer's point of view.)

___

___

___

___

___

THE FIELD TRIP

"Move over Danilou! We're both supposed to observe the wormhole," Isaac said as he shoved Danilou as hard as he could.

"I'm glad we live in the thirty-first century," Danilou commented. "I can't imagine traveling through wormholes the way the ancients did."

Danilou moved a bit to the left and Isaac leaned forward eagerly. Suddenly, his note-taker was sucked out of his hand by a **vortex** of energy and matter.

"Hey! The wormhole just stole my note-taker!" Isaac yelled.

"Well, you'll have to share with Danilou," Mr. Rodriguez said. Now it's time to continue our historical observations elsewhere."

Everyone jostled into line. Then they passed through the time-travel **portal**. Isaac turned to Danilou, "I wonder what travel will be like in the next century."

---

vortex *n.*, fast, turning, circular movement
portal *n.*, gate or doorway

Talk About It
Talk to your teacher or a classmate about the two passages and the writers' points of view.

Make the Ideas Your Own
What do you think the future will be like?

___

___

___

___

___

Ask Questions

Preview "A Break from Virtual Reality" so that you know what to expect when you read. As you read, ask and answer questions about the story and check your understanding.

Strategy at a Glance

Ask Questions

When you ask questions, you

- ask and answer questions to check your understanding
- think about the connection between questions and their answers
- think about the author's purpose and point of view.

DID YOU KNOW?

- Surgeons, pilots, and architects use virtual reality technology in their work.

A Break from Virtual Reality

Seth finished packing. He had decided to leave his personal robot for an entire weekend. He wanted to test himself. Could he get through three days without experiencing an **interactive program** on one of SimBot's networks?

"Ready," Seth said to his dad as he hopped into the hovertron. "Where's SimBot?"

"Taking a break," Seth responded.

At the campground, Seth and his dad prepared the fire ring. After a dinner of fire-roasted meat substitute and **simulated** veggie kabobs, they prepared their sleeping tents and bags.

continued on next page

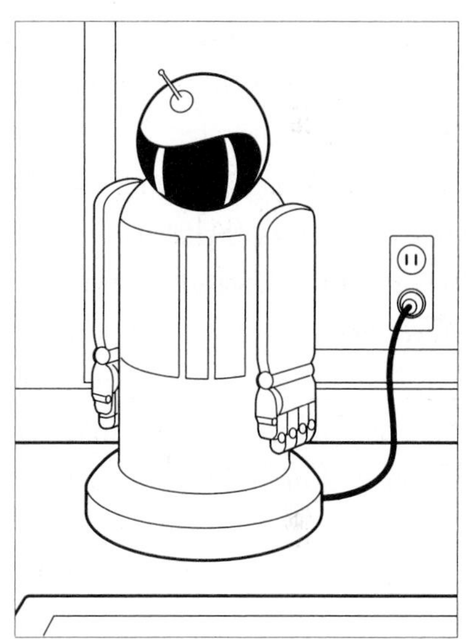

interactive program *n.,* electronic show that responds to actions of the user
simulated *adj.,* imitation

Check Your Understanding

1. When does the story take place? How can you tell?

____

____

Ask Questions

2. What questions you have about the characters.

____

____

Answer: _______________________________________

A Break from Virtual Reality, continued

Seth checked and rechecked his equipment.

"What's the matter, Seth?" his father asked.

"Oh, nothing. I'm just not used to being without SimBot," Seth admitted.

"Son, you're used to experiencing **virtual reality**. Now, enjoy the real thing." Seth's father replied.

Seth fell asleep wondering what the next day might bring. Would he be bored without his programs to interact with? Would he find real colors and sounds **inferior** to those of SimBot's programs? The **solitude** of the forest was almost overpowering. Where were all the familiar sounds of SimBot's beeps and whir-r-r-rs?

At daybreak Seth and his father ate breakfast voraciously and then began their hike into the forest. As he moved, Seth's senses began to awaken within him. Tall trees surrounded him. The warmth of the sun and the weight of his footsteps released the fragrance of pine needles on the trail. Out of habit, Seth turned to feed the information into SimBot, but then stopped himself. He did not have SimBot to interface with.

continued on next page

---

virtual reality *n.,* electronic programs that mimic real life
inferior *adj.,* not as good
solitude *n.,* being away from people

Ask Questions

3. Write a question about Seth's problem.

____

____

Answer: ____________________________________

4. Write a question about the author's attitude toward Seth.

____

____

Answer: ____________________________________

Ask Questions, continued

A Break from Virtual Reality, continued

Suddenly, Seth heard a cr-rri-ck-ack sound that reminded him of SimBot's **output**. Slowing his pace, he traced the sound to a tree. Above him, he spotted the bright red head of a woodpecker. It stopped pecking at the bark and gazed right back at him.

"Hey, you're not electronic," Seth whispered.

The bird pecked the tree a few more times and then flew away. Seth's fingers itched to push a replay button so he could study the bird again. At that moment Seth began to see reality in a new light. Reality doesn't have instant replay. You have to soak up as much as you can in every moment of experience. Suddenly life seemed very **temporary** and precious.

"Did you see that woodpecker, Dad?" Seth called.

"Nope. I must've missed it," his father replied.

"Better keep your eyes and ears open," Seth remarked. "You're likely to miss something special, if you don't."

Seth's father just smiled. "This hike is worth more than a thousand robots," he thought.

continued on next page

output *n.,* an electronic function that responds to the user
temporary *adj.,* brief, not lasting

Check Your Understanding

5. Why is Seth's advice to "keep your eyes and ears open" important?

6. What is the author's purpose in telling this story?

Ask Questions, continued

A Break from Virtual Reality, continued

At the end of the day, Seth found himself torn between remembering the day's experiences and enjoying the restful mood of the campsite. He recalled his surprise when he first saw the woodpecker and his **dismay** that he could not replay the moment. He relived the **novel** sensation of staying alert for every detail he might see, hear, smell, or feel. He could still sense the weariness of his legs after the long hike.

But now stars crowded the sky. An owl hooted and a coyote howled. A cool night breeze ruffled his hair as he crawled into his sleeping bag. "Just imagine," he thought, "what new experiences a night in a forest holds." He'd have to stay awake all night so he wouldn't miss anything.

It was then that Seth realized he hadn't thought about SimBot for hours. In his normal life, SimBot was a constant. A shift in his awareness had occurred. And he was pleased with his new outlook.

"SimBot, I made it without you," Seth said aloud, "and I think we both needed a break." Then, he fell deep asleep.

---

dismay *n.,* worry
novel *adj.,* new, unusual

Sum It Up

7. Sum up the conflict and resolution of the story. Connect the story events with an experience of your own.

____

____

____

____

Self-Assessment

8. How did asking and answering questions help you get the most out of the story?

____

____

Name ______________________ Date __________

Ask Questions

Preview "Home, Sweet Tree." Write a question about the text:

____

Ask and answer more questions as you read. Also check your understanding.

Strategy at a Glance

Ask Questions

When you ask questions, you

- ask and answer questions to check your understanding
- think about the connection between questions and their answers
- think about the author's purpose and point of view.

Home, Sweet Tree

Green Buildings Are Great

Most people have noticed green buildings around them. Green buildings are not necessarily green in color, but they are green in purpose. They are environment-friendly **structures**. Some use straw bales inside concrete shells. These houses are naturally **insulated** against heat and cold. Another way to save on heating and cooling costs is to put part of a house underground.

continued on next page

structures *n.*, buildings
insulated *adj.*, protected

Ask Questions

1. Write a question about the ideas presented in this paragraph.

____

____

Answer: ______________________________

____

2. Write another question you have.

____

____

Answer: ______________________________

____

Ask Questions, continued

Home, Sweet Tree, continued

What is a Fab Tree Hab?

One team of architects has taken green to the limit, though. They have designed a house that starts from a few tree seedlings. It grows into a water-recycling **abode** that is energy-efficient. The Fab Tree Hab, a mix of ancient and ultramodern technology, isn't merely **eco-friendly**. It *is* the environment.

Architects Mitchell Joachim and Javier Arbone discovered that in ancient times, gardeners wove together young trees into built forms, such as archways and **lattices**. The forms were strong and lasted through the years. The modern architects realized that they might apply this gardening method, or pleaching, in their home designs. They experimented by designing a living, breathing house!

continued on next page

abode *n.,* living space, home
eco-friendly *adj.,* not damaging to the environment or ecosystem
lattices *n.,* crisscrossed strips of wood or branches

Ask Questions

3. How does the information in this part of the article fit with what you know?

Answer: ______________________________

____

____

____

4. Where can you find the answer to question 3?

____

____

____

5. Write a new question about the ideas in the article.

____

____

____

____

Ask Questions, continued

Home, Sweet Tree, continued

How can builders preserve natural resources while constructing a comfortable, modern home? The main structure of the experimental house is supported by trees, such as elm, live oak, and dogwood. Builders use smaller plants like vines and branches to form a lattice. The lattice becomes the **exterior** walls and roof of the house. The **interior** walls are covered with a smooth mixture of clay and straw. This covering keeps the interior clean and dry. Inside, dwellers can expect to use modern technology.

The Fab Tree Hab is fascinating! This home is composed of 100 percent living nutrients. To the designers, the tree house idea is also a living argument against cutting down timber.

continued on next page

exterior *adj.,* outside
interior *adj.,* inside

Ask Questions

6. How does the writer feel about the Fab Tree Hab? How can you tell?

Answer: ______________________________

7. What do you think is the author's purpose in writing this article?

Answer: ______________________________

Ask Questions, continued

Home, Sweet Tree, continued

Past vs. Future

In contrast, typical building materials are manufactured. Most of these materials contain **pollutants** that can cause cancer. In addition, building a house today requires the wood of 88 trees! All those trees have to be killed to create the lumber. In other words, life is lost or damaged by traditional building methods. The designers of the Fab Tree Hab believe it is time to change our traditional thinking.

At this time, the Fab Tree Hab is still in the experimental stage. The architects insist, however, that it is a **viable** effort. They believe future homes must be able to support, not consume, natural resources. To them, the Fab Tree Hab is an example of what a future home should be like.

---

pollutants *n.,* chemical or waste products
viable *adj.,* practical, can be done

Sum It Up

8. What are the benefits of the Fab Tree Hab?

Self-Assessment

9. How did asking and answering questions help you understand the ideas presented in the selection?

Name ______________________ Date __________

Create Images for Nonfiction

Preview "Monsters of the Deep" so that you know what to expect when you read. As you read, underline words that help you create pictures in your mind.

Strategy at a Glance

Visualize

To make images in your mind, you

- study any photographs or graphics
- look for words that describe and explain things
- add your own experience and look for more facts to sharpen your focus.

DID YOU KNOW?

- The squid is related to the octopus.
- A squid's arms have sharp hooks for teeth.

Monsters of the Deep

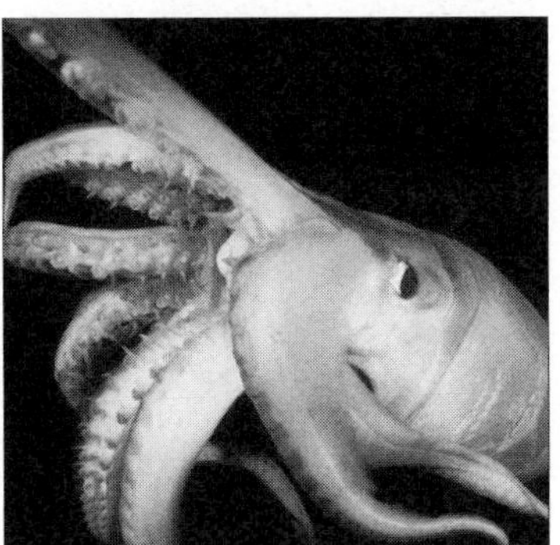

A giant squid uses its tentacles to grab a snack.

The giant squid makes its home in the deepest, darkest depths of the ocean. Does it rise up to **capsize** large ships? Will it grow to be a mile long and swallow whales whole? While squid may not live up to such legends, they are impressive creatures. In fact, squid may be the most intelligent invertebrates in the sea.

The Humboldt squid has earned the nickname "giant squid" for good reason. These intelligent creatures are physically **imposing**. They weigh up to 100 pounds. They can grow to be 7 feet long. They have eight strong arms capable of pulling large prey into their razor-sharp mouths. And they can change colors in the blink of an eye.

Scientists know the squid are great hunters. They can snatch and devour large fish in seconds. Yet experts do not agree on whether the squid pose a danger to people. Dr. William Gilley has studied Humboldt squid for more than 20 years.

continued on next page

---

capsize *v.*, tip over

imposing *adj.*, frightening and large

Draw or describe what you "see" as you read.

Monsters of the Deep, continued

He does not believe the animals are dangerous. "To the best of my knowledge there's no **documentation** that they've attacked anyone," says Gilley.

Scott Cassell, a wildlife filmmaker and diver, says that Gilley's comments make squid seem cute or harmless. Cassell strongly disagrees. "This is simply not true," he says. "I've actually seen a Humboldt squid attack a thresher shark twice its size."

Cassell has been attacked and injured several times by the animals. On one dive, a large squid **rammed** him in the chest. The attack left him with badly bruised ribs. During another dive, an angry squid grabbed him and dragged him down about 30 feet. A squid bite on his leg required twenty-five stitches.

It can be dangerous diving with Humboldt squid. For that reason, Cassell no longer dives without protection. He wears a special diving suit with chains that help protect him from the squid's sharp beaks and more than 1,200 sucker disks. Each of these disks contains as many as twenty-six razor-sharp teeth. For extra protection, Cassell has developed an "anti-squid" cage. This cage is similar to those used to protect divers from hungry sharks. Squid are definitely not imaginary creatures. They are very, very real matches for humans who enter their **domain**.

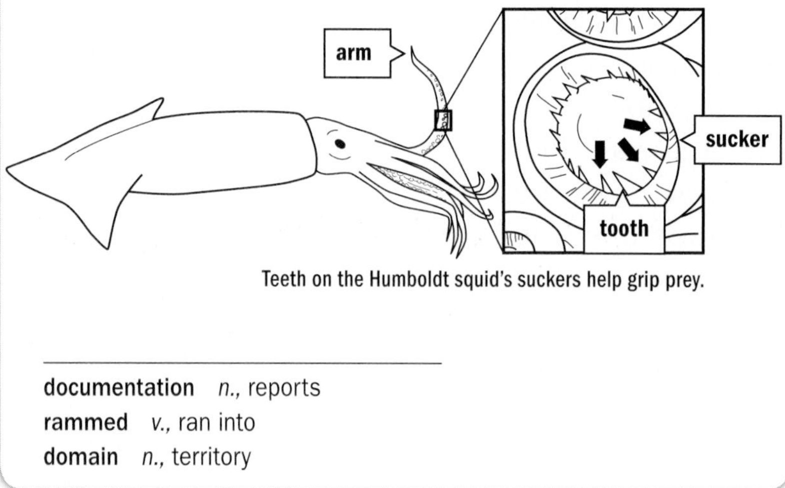

Teeth on the Humboldt squid's suckers help grip prey.

---

documentation *n.,* reports
rammed *v.,* ran into
domain *n.,* territory

Draw or describe what you "see" as you read.

Talk About It

Tell your teacher or a classmate what you pictured as you read the article.

Name ______________________ Date ______________

Create Images for Fiction

Preview "First Solo Flight" so that you know what to expect when you read. As you read, underline words that help you make a mental movie.

Strategy at a Glance

Visualize

To make a movie in your mind, you

- study illustrations and other visuals
- look for words that describe the setting, characters, and events
- add what you know from your own experience and put the pictures together like scenes in a movie.

DID YOU KNOW?

- To fly an air balloon, you must earn a special pilot's license.
- A solo flight is when a pilot flies alone.

First Solo Flight

It's still dark outside as Sandra sits in her kitchen listening to the radio. "No more snow in the forecast. Today will be sunny and clear with a cool breeze of 2–6 miles per hour." She smiles as she thinks, "A perfect day for my first solo flight in a hot air balloon."

As Sandra drives off in her truck, she notices things she will soon see from hundreds of feet above—the creek, the train tracks, the small town of Lyons built into the foothills.

At the take-off site, Sandra parks and hurries toward her crew who are already at work. They've spread the huge lime-green balloon across the snow-white field.

"You're about to see the most breathtaking views Colorado has to offer," George replies. George glances at the jagged, snow-capped Rocky Mountains. Then he turns toward the **vast** Colorado plains.

continued on next page

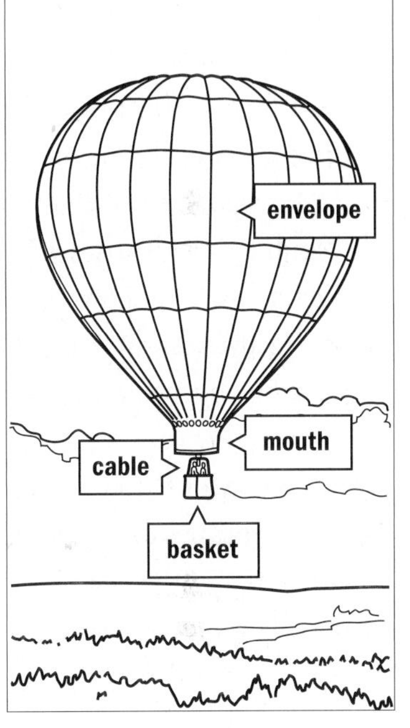

vast *adj.*, covering a large area

Draw or describe what you see so far. Then keep reading on the next page.

First Solo Flight, continued

"You'll be able to see all the way to Kansas!" Elliot adds.

Sandra pulls on her gloves and starts working on the huge basket resting on its side. She hooks it to the envelope with twenty colored cables. She **secures** the compass and flight instruments on board. The crewmembers open up the mouth of the balloon and start the fan. As the huge envelope fills with air, George and Andy check for any rips.

"Everything's in good shape," Andy says. "Are you nervous?"

"Of course I am."

Sandra gives the gas burner a quick blast. The crew **flinches** with the loud roar of the flame. The air inside the balloon grows warmer, and the balloon begins to rise. The envelope tugs hard at the ropes holding it down. Elliot turns the basket upright, and Sandra climbs in. At her signal, the crewmembers release the basket.

Sandra quickly rises up. Her lime-green balloon casts a giant shadow across the snow. To the west, the Rocky Mountains unfold before her eyes. To the east, the flat plains seem to stretch out forever. She **fires** the burner and rises higher to catch a northern wind. Sandra catches her breath when she sees the brilliant blue sky cut sharply against the white ground. She will meet her crew at the landing site. In the meantime, she'll enjoy her bird's-eye view of the world.

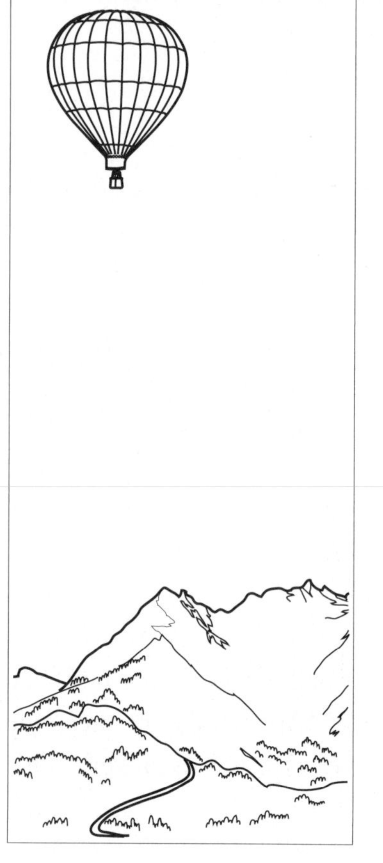

---

secures *v.,* locks or ties down
flinches *v.,* jumps back suddenly
fires *v.,* turns up the flame

Draw or describe other scenes in your mental movie.

Talk About It

Tell your teacher or a classmate about your mental movie.

Name ______________________ Date __________

Have a Virtual Experience

Preview "A Great Escape" so that you know what to expect when you read. As you read the article, underline the words that help you use your senses to experience what the writer is describing.

Strategy at a Glance

Visualize

To experience what you read, you

- notice words that appeal to your senses and create mental pictures
- add your own experience
- use your imagination to fill in pictures.

DID YOU KNOW?

- Harry Houdini began performing escape acts in the 1890s.
- He was famous in America, Europe, and Australia.

A Great Escape

Houdini performs his famous "milk can escape."

Harry Houdini, the great escape artist, stood on a stage before an eager audience. Everyone was ready to see his famous "milk can escape." He was about to be locked into a padlocked metal container filled with water. Today, we know that his escape was an **illusion**. But waiting for Houdini to emerge before drowning would make anyone's heart race. This trick took tremendous **endurance**.

Houdini climbed into the small metal **canister**. There was just enough room for him if he curled up tight. The water was so cold that his muscles started to cramp. As the lid was jammed on, he took a last, deep breath. Then he was plunged into inky darkness. Water in his ears distorted the sounds of locks snapping and a screen being positioned to hide the audience's view.

continued on next page

illusion *n.,* a trick of the eye
endurance *n.,* the body's ability to stand extreme conditions
canister *n.,* container

Describe your own experience and what you imagine.

Continue reading the article and underlining words that help you use your senses to experience what the writer is describing.

A Great Escape, continued

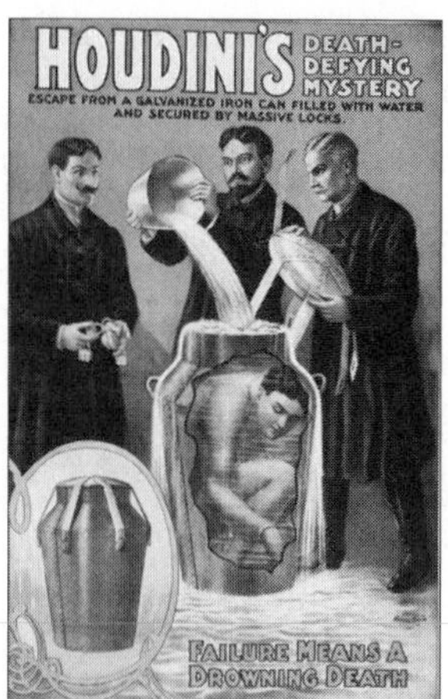

Poster advertising a Houdini performance

Cold metal pressed in on all sides. Houdini's lungs felt as if they were on fire. He tilted his face and inhaled the stale air that was trapped under the lid. That bit of air would give him the extra seconds he needed.

Time was running out. Straining every muscle, he pushed up with his shoulders and head. Nothing. He pushed harder, beginning to panic. Finally, the top came loose. The milk can looked solid, but he knew it actually came apart. Fake **rivets** on the container made the trick possible. Trembling with relief, he climbed out and prepared for the grand **finale**. The screen was removed. He bowed, dripping and gasping. The audience cheered. Once more, Houdini had tested his endurance. The next day he would test it again and astonish another audience.

For years, Houdini had challenged himself physically. He had developed many different techniques for getting out of ropes and straightjackets, not to mention handcuffs and chains. He had practiced holding his breath until he could do so for more than three minutes. He had even taught himself to untie knots with his toes.

Houdini invented many illusions. If someone copied one of his stunts, he designed a harder one. During his long career, Houdini broke, injured, or sprained nearly every part of his body. Houdini continued to perform until his death in 1926.

---

rivets *n.,* metal fasteners
finale *n.,* ending of a performance

Describe your own experience and what you imagine.

Talk About It

Tell your teacher or a classmate what you imagined as you read about Houdini's milk can escape.

Name ______________________ Date ____________

Read and Respond

Preview "The Polar Bear Plunge" so that you know what to expect when you read. As you read the text, underline words to help track how you feel.

Strategy at a Glance

Visualize

To track how you feel, you

- notice words that describe people, places, and events to create mental pictures
- think about how those words and pictures make you feel
- identify the specific words and phrases that led to those feelings.

DID YOU KNOW?

- In February, the temperature of Lake Ontario is often between 30 and 35 degrees.

The Polar Bear Plunge

People enjoying the Polar Bear Plunge

For many people, summer is the best time of year. But I wait for the winter, particularly the month of February. In my hometown of Rochester, New York, February brings day after day of frosty weather. Instead of hitting the slopes, I head for the water. I dress up in a wacky costume and **plunge** into the icy waters of Lake Ontario. And I'm not alone. Hundreds of others participate in the yearly Polar Bear Plunge.

Dozens of cities across the country organize their own Polar Bear Plunges to raise money for the Special Olympics. The Special Olympics is an **annual** sporting event that gives developmentally challenged youth a chance to play sports and have fun. For the Polar Bear Plunge, sponsors donate money to the Special Olympics. In return, participants agree to put on **zany** costumes and go for a brisk winter swim.

continued on next page

---

plunge *n.,* jump
annual *adj.,* yearly
zany *adj.,* crazy, silly

Draw or describe how you feel so far. Then keep reading on the next page.

Continue to read the passage and underline words to help track how you feel.

The Polar Bear Plunge, continued

Participants wear fun costumes for the plunge.

I'll never forget the first time I waded into the bone-chilling waters of Lake Ontario. I was dressed as a pirate. People who came to support the swimmers sported heavy coats, boots, gloves, and scarves because it was so cold. We saw ice chunks floating around in the water! I was scared. What if my body went into shock? Or worse, what if I backed out once I touched the freezing water? How could I ever face myself after that?

When it was time to take the plunge, we let out a **collective** cheer. Before I knew it, I was neck deep in the water, pushing away chunks of ice with my pirate sword. Surprisingly, the water wasn't that bad. My body turned numb and I couldn't feel much. The worst part was getting over the fear and taking that first step.

Everyone participates in the plunge for different reasons. What helped me take that first step? I remembered the look on my brother Sammy's face when he hit his first baseball in the Special Olympics. It was a look of complete and **utter** happiness. I'll be taking the Polar Bear Plunge every year. In fact, I would swim the length of Lake Ontario to see that expression on Sammy's face.

---

collective *adj.,* all together
utter *adj.,* total, complete

Draw or describe how you feel.

Talk About It

Talk to your teacher or a classmate about your mental pictures and how those pictures made you feel.

Name ______________________ Date ____________

Visualize

Preview "Dancing to Victory" so that you know what to expect when you read. As you read, create pictures in your mind and use all your senses.

Strategy at a Glance

Visualize

When you visualize, you

- notice descriptions and add what you know from your life to create mental pictures
- look for words that tell how things look, sound, smell, taste, and feel.

DID YOU KNOW?

- Ballet can improve an athlete's precision, coordination, and balance.
- Ballet training is extremely physically challenging.

DANCING TO VICTORY

Saby Benga gripped the smooth wooden **barre** with his left hand, his right dangling awkwardly at his side. *Just my luck to be in high school when Coach has the craziest idea of his entire career,* Saby thought.

"First position!" Miss Cheri instructed. "Heels together and toes out!"

The Spartans had to win their regional conference, and Saby was the best wide receiver the team had had in years. Even so, Saby needed to improve his **agility** or the Spartans had no hope for victory. Coach Porter had an **unconventional** approach: ballet lessons.

continued on next page

barre *n.,* handrail that ballet dancers hold for balance during practice
agility *n.,* ability to move quickly and smoothly
unconventional *adj.,* odd, not traditional

Check Your Understanding

1. Who is Saby Benga?

____

____

2. What is his problem?

____

____

Visualize, continued

Dancing to Victory, continued

Saby had rejected the idea, but he hadn't argued. He remembered how, in the last game, he had been tackled over and over by his opponents. He wished he had his friend Len's ability to change direction in an instant. Len seemed able to **wriggle** out of any tackle, unless several players ganged up on him. He had seen how that kind of agility had resulted in Len's two touchdowns. So, Saby took Coach's direction in silence.

Now, he was surrounded by shiny mirrors and posters of leaping dancers. All around him, both male and female dancers seemed to float through the air. They could land facing one direction and suddenly take off at a **90-degree angle**. *How do they do that?* he wondered.

On the football field Saby knew what to do. He knew exactly how to plant his feet to be ready for a mad dash downfield. In this dance studio, he felt completely out of place. He had no idea how to position his feet to make the moves the instructor demanded. He felt like a **paralyzed** gorilla. But at least he was a determined gorilla.

continued on next page

---

wriggle *v.,* wiggle and squirm
90-degree angle *n.,* square corner
paralyzed *adj.,* unable to move

Visualize

3. Compare how Saby and Len look when they play football. Draw or describe.

Visualize, continued

Dancing to Victory, continued

"**Plié**, right arm out. Eyes forward. Follow my lead."

Saby stood frozen. The teacher paused. "Caryn, please assist Saby."

Caryn approached the football player. She seemed so delicate during school, but now he realized that she was muscular and athletic.

"What does this have to do with football?" Saby growled **apprehensively**. He would have given all his trophies to be back on the field.

"Saby, I know you think you don't belong in a dance studio. But you'll be happy with the results if you learn this stuff. It really will give you more agility on the football field." Caryn said. "Forget your feelings and just concentrate on the positions of your feet."

Saby focused on Caryn's feet and moved his to **approximate** her positions as well as he could. He felt unbalanced at first, but became more comfortable as he bent his knees, following Caryn's lead.

"You're getting it," Caryn encouraged. "Do a few more of those before we move on to something more challenging."

continued on next page

---

plié *v.,* bend your knees
apprehensively *adv.,* with fear
approximate *v.,* copy almost exactly

Check Your Understanding

4. How does Saby feel in the dance studio? How can you tell?

___

___

___

Monitor Your Reading

5. What do you predict will happen next?

___

___

___

Visualize, continued

Dancing to Victory, continued

"What do you mean 'more challenging'?" Saby asked. He didn't like the sound of that at all!

With her left foot in front of her right, Caryn jumped, fluttered both feet in mid-air, and landed on one foot with delicate **precision**.

Saby **observed** how her foot met the ground. It seemed to melt into the ground, and her muscles fought gravity every second. He pictured himself landing after a catch just the way Caryn had. Then quickly shifting direction to streak past his opponents. Suddenly he wanted to learn whatever he could from ballet. He imagined showing the guys on the field his new moves. He could feel Coach's pride.

"Now you try," Caryn directed.

Saby placed his left foot in front of his right and pushed off. But his shaky legs buckled, and he landed with a thud. *How could my legs be tired from just this little workout?* he mused. His face burned with shame.

"It's hard," Saby admitted. Then he rose to his full height. "But I'm trying that one again," he said.

---

precision *n.,* exactness
observed *v.,* watched

Visualize

6. Describe and draw your mental movie of "Dancing to Victory."

Self-Assessment

7. How did visualizing add to your enjoyment of the story? Give examples.

____

____

Name ______________________ Date ____________

Visualize

Preview "Take a Deep Breath—and Climb!" so that you know what to expect when you read. As you read, create pictures in your mind.

Strategy at a Glance

Visualize

When you visualize, you

- use the writer's words to create mental pictures
- look for words that tell how things look, sound, smell, taste, and feel
- add in your own experiences.

DID YOU KNOW?

- Lung disease is the fourth leading cause of death.
- The average runner scales the John Hancock Center in Chicago in 26 minutes.

TAKE A DEEP BREATH—AND CLIMB!

Hustle Up the Hancock

Imagine you and 4,000 others are climbing stairs to the top of a Chicago skyscraper. Your lungs burn. Your heart pounds. Your knees pump. Why would so many people make this effort? These climbers raise money for the American Lung Association. The event, **dubbed** "Hustle Up the Hancock," is the largest fundraiser for the Association in the city of Chicago.

John Hancock Center in Chicago, Illinois

continued on next page

dubbed *v.,* called

Check Your Understanding

1. What is the main idea of this paragraph?

____

____

Visualize

2. Which words and phrases from this paragraph help you create mental pictures?

____

____

Visualize, continued

Take a Deep Breath—and Climb!, continued

The Event

For over ten years, the John Hancock Center has set aside a day for participants in the event to climb to the top. Organizers remind climbers that this event is a 1,000-foot **vertical** hike to the 94th floor of the Hancock skyscraper.

Participants in the event form teams to help each other on the way up. When a team member tires from the **strain** of climbing, the rest of the team cheers the **flagging** climber on. It doesn't really matter who gets to the top of the 1,632 stairs the fastest. What does matter is that all the climbers finish. Each climber has several sponsors. The sponsors donate money to the Association if the climber finishes.

continued on next page

vertical *adj.,* straight up
strain *n.,* struggle
flagging *adj.,* tiring out

Check Your Understanding

3. How do teams help each climber?

____

____

4. How is this event similar to and different from other races you have seen or read about?

____

____

____

____

Visualize

5. What experiences from your life help you imagine what the writer is describing?

____

____

____

Visualize, continued

Take a Deep Breath—and Climb!, continued

Why Climb?

The purpose of the "Hustle" is to support medical research that studies treatments for lung disease. Similar fundraisers for the American Lung Association are held across the country throughout the year. The "Hustle," however, is the only one that involves climbing the Hancock Center.

For many, the day is more than a physical strain. It is an extremely emotional day. Typically, participants form groups in memory of someone who has suffered from lung cancer. Many of these racers are themselves lung cancer survivors. Their relatives and friends often are climbing right there with them. Others have had an organ transplant operation. They know that without the organ donation from an **altruistic** person, they might not have survived to make the climb.

continued on next page

altruistic *adj.*, unselfish, caring about others

Check Your Understanding

6. Why do people participate in "Hustle Up the Hancock"?

7. Why is the day of the race so emotional?

Visualize, continued

Take a Deep Breath—and Climb!, continued

The Finish Line

The finish line for the event is on the top floor. Friends and families of the participants go up the easy way. They take an elevator and wait to congratulate the climbers.

Just as mountain climbers look at the stunning views when they get to a **summit**, these racers have the Hancock **observation deck**. From there, they look down on the whole city of Chicago.

For many reasons, these participants feel like they are on top of the world. By participating in "Hustle Up the Hancock," they have helped others reflect on their health. They've shown how everyone can contribute to the fight against lung disease.

---

summit *n.,* top of a mountain
observation deck *n.,* flat place with a large view

Visualize

8. Describe or draw the finish line as you imagined it.

9. How do these mental pictures make you feel?

Self-Assessment

10. How did visualizing help you understand the selection?

Name ______________________ Date __________

Link to Your Experience

Preview "An Open Book" so that you know what to expect when you read. As you read, link the text to your experience.

Strategy at a Glance

Make Connections

To link to your experience, you

- think about what you know about the topic from your own life
- think about what the ideas and events in the text remind you of
- ask how your own experience helps you understand the text.

An Open Book

Would you read your diary aloud to a group of strangers?

You are sorting through a box of your junior high photos, when you come across your old diary. You flip through the pages and chuckle. Those were some embarrassing times! Can you imagine reading your diary out loud, to a room full of strangers?

Some people can. They perform in wildly popular stage shows with real people sharing real stories. But these are not just any stories. On stage, people return to the past. They can't wait to share their **naïve** anecdotes. They read aloud their childhood diaries, love letters, or poems. The performers read about fights with mom, childhood illnesses, and why they deserve to marry Bon Jovi.

Why would someone share a private diary with the world? Robert Thompson, a pop-culture expert, says people experience feelings of connection and belonging when they share happy, sad, or **humiliating** stories. Laughing with others helps people recall the way they felt when an embarrassing incident happened and get beyond it.

continued on next page

1. What I know about the topic:

2. What the events and ideas in the text remind me of:

3. How my experience helps me understand the text:

---

naïve *adj.*, immature and innocent

humiliating *adj.*, very embarrassing

Continue to read the passage and link to your experience.

An Open Book, continued

Thompson notes that students now deal with embarrassing situations much differently than when he was in school. Back then, Thompson says, one embarrassing moment could **wreck** your entire school experience. Now students are able to share their stories and deal with the experiences in healthier ways. He believes that "The tendency and desire to talk about ourselves has overcome the feeling of embarrassment. Everybody forgets it." Sharing a humiliating story can be **cathartic**.

The staged performances help people deal with embarrassment. It's good to know that other people can **empathize** with your fears and **tribulations**—that they've been through similar experiences. Dealing with the embarrassment is half the battle of getting over it. And it's a great way to get a laugh.

wreck *v.*, destroy
cathartic *adj.*, healing
empathize *v.*, feel the same way as someone else
tribulations *n.*, problems

1. What I know about the topic:

2. What the events and ideas in the text remind me of:

3. How my experience helps me understand the text:

Talk About It

Review your notes. Use them to tell your teacher or a classmate how your experience helped you understand the text.

Make the Ideas Your Own

How has this article changed your thinking? What do you know now about how humor affects people?

Name ________________________ Date ____________

Connect to What You Already Know

Preview "After Career Day" so that you know what to expect when you read. As you read, link the ideas to what you already know.

Strategy at a Glance

Make Connections

To connect a writer's ideas to real life, you

- think about what you already know about the topic
- think about what the text reminds you of from the world around you
- stop to ask yourself how what you already know adds to your understanding of the text.

DID YOU KNOW?

- Six percent of nurses in the U.S. are men.
- Most hospitals in the U.S. have a shortage of registered nurses.

1. The topic is:

____

____

2. What I already know about the topic:

____

____

____

____

3. What the text reminds me of:

____

____

____

____

4. How what I know adds to my understanding of the story:

____

____

____

____

____

____

____

After Career Day

"Well, Steve," his mother said as the family sat down to dinner. "How was career day at school? Did you find something you'd like to do?"

"I think so," Steven answered. "There were some interesting speakers and a lot of good choices."

"Well, don't leave us in **suspense**. What did you decide?" his father urged.

"Yeah, Stevie," his little sister Donnella piped up. "What are you going to be when you grow up?"

"Well," Steven began slowly. "There was this guy from the local hospital. He talked about this great **profession** and said that there are lots of possibilities for someone who is willing to work hard. He was talking about nursing."

"Nursing?" His mother stopped sipping water and put her glass down carefully.

"A nurse?" His father raised an eyebrow.

"A boy nurse?" His sister giggled. "Boys can't be nurses."

"Who says?" Steven asked, glaring at his sister. "Boys—men can be nurses, too. Nurses work just as hard as doctors do and they deal with patients more often."

continued on next page

suspense *n.,* waiting for an answer
profession *n.,* career

5. What the text reminds me of from the world around me:

6. How what I know adds to my understanding:

Talk About It
Tell your teacher or a classmate how making connections to the real world helped you understand the text.

Make the Ideas Your Own
Has this article changed your thinking about jobs for men? Explain why or why not.

After Career Day, continued

Everyone fell silent. Steven's dad sawed **intently** at the roast, and speared a large slice with a fork. Steven looked down at his undisturbed plate, picking at the mashed potatoes. He wondered why his parents didn't seem to get it.

"What else are you **considering**?" his father asked, looking at Steven.

"Nothing." Steven shrugged. "Nursing is what I want to do."

His father sighed. Steven leaned toward him.

"Dad, if Donnella said she wanted to be a doctor, you wouldn't be upset, would you? You wouldn't be unhappy about her career choice. Well, there's nothing wrong with me wanting to become a nurse. There's nothing wrong with . . . "

"He's right," Steven's mother broke in suddenly. "After all, think about when I had gall bladder surgery. The nurse spent more time with me than the doctor did."

His father stopped eating, remembering his wife's surgery, and how painful it was for him, too. He looked squarely at his son. "Steven, I'll be proud when you become a nurse," he said.

---

intently *adv.*, with focused attention
considering *v.*, thinking about

Name ______________________ Date ____________

Form New Knowledge

Preview the newspaper article below so that you know what to expect when you read. As you read, take note of new ideas and information.

Strategy at a Glance

Make Connections

To form new knowledge as you read, you

- think about what you already know
- notice new ideas and information
- pause to ask how the new knowledge fits with what you already know.

DID YOU KNOW?

- Being obese, or seriously overweight, causes many health problems, including high blood pressure, heart disease, some cancers, and diabetes.
- Behavior and environment play a large role causing people to be overweight and obese.

1. What I know about the topic before reading:

____

____

____

____

____

2. New ideas and information from the text:

____

____

____

____

____

____

____

3. How the new information fits with what I know:

____

____

____

____

____

____

____

As Obesity Rates Rise, Schools Reconsider Vending-Machine Contracts

by Camille Ricketts

Nov. 2—WASHINGTON—Juvenile obesity rates may begin at home, but thousands of U.S. schools have signed contracts that feed the growing problem.

Over half of all high schools and junior high schools nationwide have struck deals with soft-drink companies or vendors, giving them **exclusive** marketing rights to their students, according to the Institute of Medicine, a health policy advisor to Congress. In exchange, the schools often get five- or six-figure payments that cover benefits their budgets don't, such as SAT test fees for low-income students, new scoreboards, uniforms and even proms.

The problem is that the marketing deals often promote **consumption** of foods that are a nutritionist's nightmare. Pennsylvania school food-service directors, for example, reported in June that their cafeterias' best sellers were, in rank order: pizza, hamburgers, and sandwiches; cookies, crackers, cakes, and pastries; french fries; potato chips and cheese puffs; and sodas and sugary sports drinks.

Since, according to the institute's study, 40 percent of kids' daily food intake occurs while they're at school, schools are implicated in a worrisome trend: Childhood obesity has doubled among teens and tripled for kids ages 6 to 11 since the 1970s. That's according to the Institute of Medicine's study, "Preventing Childhood Obesity," which was released Sept. 30.

continued on next page

exclusive *adj.* sole, or single
consumption *n.,* the eating

Form New Knowledge, continued

As you read the rest of the article, continue asking yourself what is new to you.

4. New ideas and information from the text:

____

____

____

____

____

5. How the new information fits with what I know:

____

____

____

____

____

____

Make the Ideas Your Own

What new ideas do you have about obesity rates and vending machines at school?

____

____

____

____

____

____

____

____

____

____

____

____

As Obesity Rates Rise..., continued

School meals served as part of the National Lunch and Breakfast programs aren't the problem. Schools must provide specified amounts of vitamins and nutrients to be **reimbursed** by the Department of Agriculture under these programs. Rather, it's food sold in vending machines and lunchtime a la carte lines that often has no nutritional standard and is intended to be popular—and profitable.

The cafeteria at George Washington Middle School, in Silver Spring, Md., has been trying to serve healthier entrees.

At Montgomery-Blair, a school that's trying—largely in vain—to shift student tastes toward healthful fare, nutritional value isn't what sells food, according to students.

"It's really just what's available and what tastes good," said Elena Pinsky, a junior. "We get **inundated** with information about healthy eating, the food pyramid and whatever, but in the end you can choose whether or not to listen and most people don't."

Senior Nick Falgout agreed. "Kids just don't see how what they eat now will affect them in the immediate short term, so they don't really pay attention," he said. A case in point, Falgout noted, was his own lunch of a sugary popcorn snack.

---

reimbursed *v.*, paid back money
inundated *v.*, overwhelmed

Name ______________________ Date ____________

Link Texts by the Ideas

Preview "Home Sweet Home" and "Ready for a Change" so that you know what to expect when you read. As you read, compare the writers' ideas.

Strategy at a Glance

Make Connections

When you link texts by the ideas, you

- think about other texts you have read on the same topic
- ask if the ideas in the texts are the same or different
- ask how ideas from other texts add to your understanding of this text.

DID YOU KNOW?

- About 11% of the people who live in the U.S. were born in other countries.
- Many U.S. cities have neighborhoods with ethnic markets and restaurants.

Home Sweet Home

My name is Nour. I was born in Egypt. I like New York, and I know that moving here was **imperative** for my dad's career. But when I think about my life in Egypt, I really miss it.

There is a market in Queens that sells pita, saffron, cumin, tahini—all the ingredients we need, but they're not as good as they were in Egypt. My mom tries to make humus, babaghanoush, lamb and fig dishes. So at home, the tastes and smells are the same as they were in Aswan.

We have met many Muslim people here. It's not going to be hard for us to **assimilate**. But I'm glad that we have the opportunity to speak Arabic as often as we speak English. My grandmother doesn't understand English, and if I forgot our language, how could I talk with her? Before we left Egypt, all I could think about was the United States. I'm glad I'm here, but I will not let our life in Egypt fade away.

imperative *adj.*, very important or necessary
assimilate *v.*, blend into a new place or culture

Ready for a Change

My name is Loc. I was born in Vietnam but now I live in New York City.

The minute I arrived, I said, "Hello, Uncle Sam! Meet your new nephew!" I e-mailed photos to my friends back in Vietnam of all my new jeans and shirts. They couldn't believe how cool I look. I love the action movies here, and the hip-hop, the fast food, and the **trendy** fashions—everything!

Here you can become anything you want. I want to go into advertising. I'm so **intrigued** by the ads here. They're everywhere and really artistic. Of course, I will do well in high school. Then I will attend an art school in Chicago.

Sure, I miss my friends, and the things we used to do in Ho Chi Minh City. But I want to learn new ways and do new things. Being in the United States has opened me up to a fantastic future I had never even imagined.

trendy *adj.*, stylish
intrigued *adj.*, very interested

Topic: ______________________

____

Ideas in this text: ______________________

____

Topic: ______________________

____

Ideas in this text: ______________________

____

Now use the diagram to connect the writers' ideas.

Y Diagram

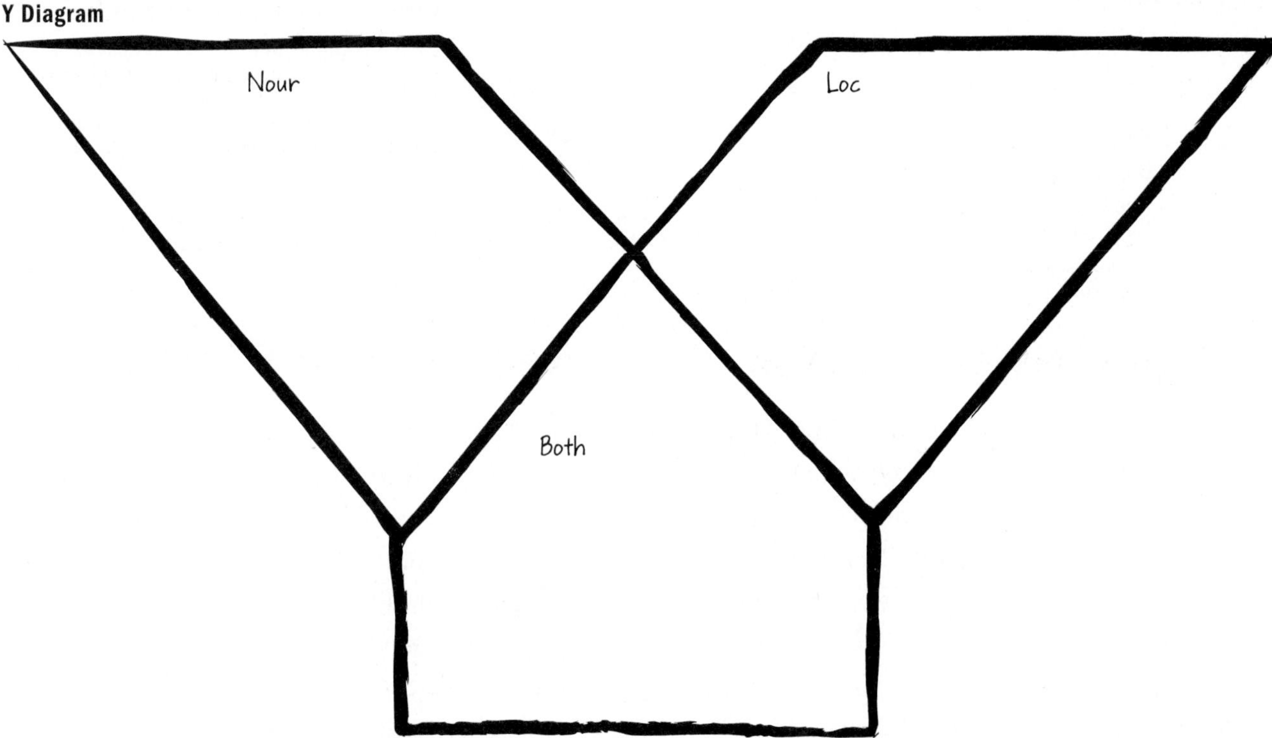

Talk About It

Tell a classmate about the two passages. Compare the writers' ideas.

Make the Ideas Your Own

How do the ideas in other texts you have read about teen immigrants add to your understanding of these texts?

Name ______________________ Date ____________

Link Texts by the Author's Style

Preview "Lost Identity" so that you know what to expect when you read. As you read, note the author's style.

Strategy at a Glance

Make Connections

When you link texts by the author's style, you

- think about the style the author used in other texts you've read
- notice whether the author uses the style you were expecting
- use your knowledge of the author's style to guide your reading.

DID YOU KNOW?

- Our sense of identity is tied to our memories.
- Identical twins have the same DNA, so they often have similar talents.

LOST IDENTITY

— Kevin Kilroy

Jason doesn't remember his brother. But then again, he doesn't remember anyone. Including himself. He disappeared one night; he hasn't been the same since. The police found him wandering the neighborhood, rubbing his head. They said Jason seemed "confused." He couldn't remember his name or address. Luckily, Jason had his driver's license with him. The doctors say Jason has **amnesia**. They don't know when he'll have his memory back. So for now, he lives with his family as strangers.

Every day Jason's brother shows him photos from their musical performances, but his eyes never awaken with remembrance. Imagine his family's surprise to wake up in the middle of the night to the sound of someone playing the piano. A lovely song, but completely different from the style he played before the night he disappeared. After the last note, his hands dropped from the keys, as if the song was the echo from someone else's past.

---

amnesia *n.,* complete or partial memory loss

Read the passage again and analyze the author's style.

Questions About the Author's Style	
1. Does the author use formal or informal language?	
2. Are the sentences short or long?	
3. What is the author's attitude like?	
4. Is the writing serious or does it make fun of something?	

This story was written by the same author. Use what you know about his style to guide your reading.

Twin Identity

— Kevin Kilroy

Up until the age of fourteen, the twins were identical in **tastes** and appearance. Teachers, coaches, and even relatives couldn't tell them apart. But on the day of their fourteenth birthday Jennifer made a decision that she did not talk over with Sarah. She sneaked away for a few hours in the afternoon and cut off all her long hair. When Sarah saw this, she became **envious** of her sister's new look. The next day, Sarah dyed her hair red—a dark, mysterious red. Imagine their friends' surprise when they showed up at the movie theater that night! One of the boys didn't believe they were sisters. Everybody was sad that Jennifer and Sarah were no longer identical.

"Why?" the sisters asked, "why?"

"Because you two were the only twins we knew."

The twins looked at each other, **suspicious** of their new identities, feeling they had stepped into somebody else's lives.

---

tastes *n.*, likes and dislikes
envious *adj.*, jealous
suspicious *adj.*, unsure

Write about how you used your knowledge of the author's style to guide your reading.

____

____

____

Talk About It

Tell your teacher how linking texts by the author's style helped you understand the selections.

Make the Ideas Your Own

What do you think makes you "you"? Is it your appearance, your family, or other things? Explain your answer.

____

____

Name ______________________ Date __________

Link Texts by the Genre

Preview "Dressed for Success." Use what you know about the genre to predict what it will be like.

Strategy at a Glance

Make Connections

When you link texts by genre, you

- preview the text to figure out if it is fiction or nonfiction
- think about what specific genre it is, such as a mystery or news article
- keep in mind the author's purpose and use the special features of the genre to stay focused.

DID YOU KNOW?

- Approximately 400 women served as soldiers during the Civil War.
- Those women had to disguise themselves as men.

1. Before you read:

What I notice about the text:

Major genre:

Genre:

Author's Purpose:

Special features I expect:

____

____

____

____

2. After you read:

How linking by genre helped me understand the text:

____

____

____

____

Dressed for Success

When I was 17, I was fed up. I'd had enough of being poor, jobless, and living on our farm at the edge of the frontier. So I journeyed on foot to a river town. I had it in mind to work on a **barge**. In exchange for my mother's **brooch**, a boatman gave me work clothes. I put them on and presented myself to the boss.

Two years later another boatman told me that I would earn much more as a soldier. I went with him the next day to **enlist** in the Union Army.

"Name and age," the officer barked.

"Joseph Edwards, 21 years old," I replied, keeping my eyes steady as my lies rolled out like honey.

"Welcome to the Union Army, boy!" The officer gave me a rough handshake and handed me a uniform. I sighed with relief. The last two years had taught me a few things. If I ducked the truth once in a while, fought bravely for my country, and wore pants, no one would guess my true identity: Mary Edwards, age 19.

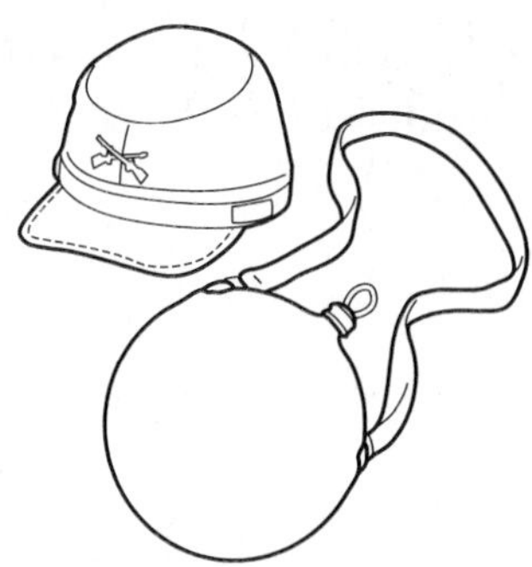

barge *n.*, large boat
brooch *n.*, decorative pin
enlist *v.*, sign up for military service

Preview "The Limping Lady." Use what you know about the genre to predict what it will be like.

DID YOU KNOW?

- The U.S., England, and the Soviet Union were allies during World War II.

1. Before you read:

What I notice about the text:

Major genre:

Genre:

Author's Purpose:

Special features I expect:

2. After you read:

How linking by genre helped me understand the text:

Make the Ideas Your Own

What do you know now about women soldiers that you didn't know before?

The Limping Lady

A Life-Changing Accident

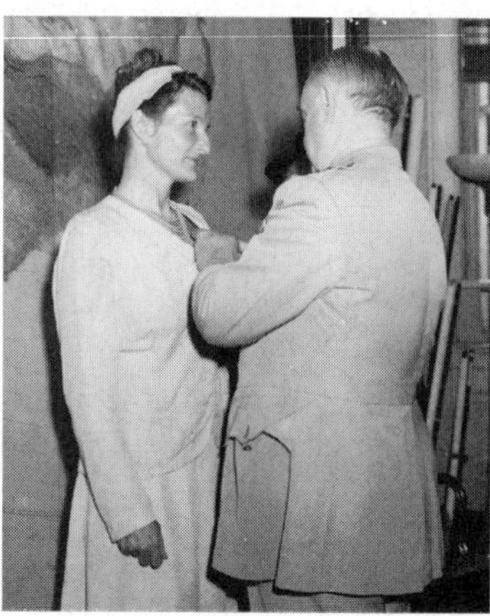

"The Limping Lady" receives the Distinguished Service Cross.

In 1933, Virginia Hall lost her leg in a hunting accident. Because of her injury, she knew her job was gone as well. Hall had been employed by the U.S. State Department in Europe. The Department had a regulation against employing **amputees**. Hall turned her disability into a powerful identity. She became "The Limping Lady," the World War II spy whom the Nazis feared.

A Spy's Life

During her career, Virginia Hall worked for a British intelligence agency and the American Office of Strategic Services. She spoke French, German, and Italian. Hall also used several aliases. Some of her aliases were Bridgette, Marie, Philomène, Germaine, and Camille.

Hall did some of her most daring work in France. There she disguised herself as an old peasant woman. She hid her telltale limp with padding and full skirts. In this disguise, Hall reported on the troop movements of the German army.

After the War

When the war was over, the United States awarded Virginia Hall the Distinguished Service Cross in honor of her courage. Hall requested a private ceremony. She wanted to keep her identity a secret.

---

amputees *n.*, people who have had an arm or leg removed

Name ______________________ Date ____________

Make Connections

Preview "A Sweet Tradition" so that you know what to expect when you read. As you read, make connections to ideas, other texts, and your own experiences.

Strategy at a Glance

Make Connections

When you make connections, you

- tap into what you know about the topic and pay attention to what the selection reminds you of
- link what you're reading to your own experiences, things you know about the world, and other texts you've read.

DID YOU KNOW?

- During World War II, 120,000 Japanese-Americans were forced into internment camps in the U.S.
- The conditions in the camps were awful.

A SWEET TRADITION

Ken stood at his kitchen counter and reached for a juicy strawberry. He had always loved strawberries and waited eagerly each year for the best crop. He felt deeply connected to strawberries for some reason. It wasn't just their delicious sweetness.

Ken inhaled the fresh **fragrance** of the fruit and memories began to surface. Vividly, he saw his grandmother and a favorite treat she used to make for him. He remembered watching her dust her hands with the starch and then roll the **mochi** into flattened pancakes. He would wait patiently as she wrapped the dough around a ripened strawberry.

continued on next page

---

fragrance *n.*, pleasant smell or aroma
mochi *n.*, sticky rice paste

Check Your Understanding

1. What reminds Ken of his grandmother? Why?

____

____

____

Make Connections

2. What connection can you make with Ken's experience so far?

____

____

Make Connections, continued

A Sweet Tradition, continued

Ken turned the strawberry in his hand. He fondly remembered his grandmother's kitchen. It was such a warm and cozy place. He remembered learning to "cook Japanese" there. He remembered a typical conversation that flowed around him as he absorbed his grandmother's teachings.

"Good work, Kenjirou-kun," **Oba-san** said approvingly.

"His name is Ken," my mother **reproved**. "Mom, this week you already showed him how to cook squid. Are you going to demonstrate how to make those rice balls now? Next thing I know, my son won't like my cooking any more!"

"Linda, he wants to learn. He's proud of who he is," Ken's grandmother argued gently. Linda shrugged and picked up her briefcase. She had to meet her clients soon. Ken was secretly glad when she had to work. It meant more time for him to eat good things from his grandmother's kitchen. Not that his mother didn't make good things, too. Her chocolate chip cookies couldn't be beat. But there was something about the old ways that fascinated Ken.

continued on next page

Oba-san *n.*, Japanese word for "Grandmother"
reproved *v.*, scolded

Check Your Understanding

3. What does the conversation tell you about Ken's mother and grandmother?

____

____

Make Connections

4. How can you connect the story with your own ideas and experiences?

____

____

____

____

Make Connections, continued

A Sweet Tradition, continued

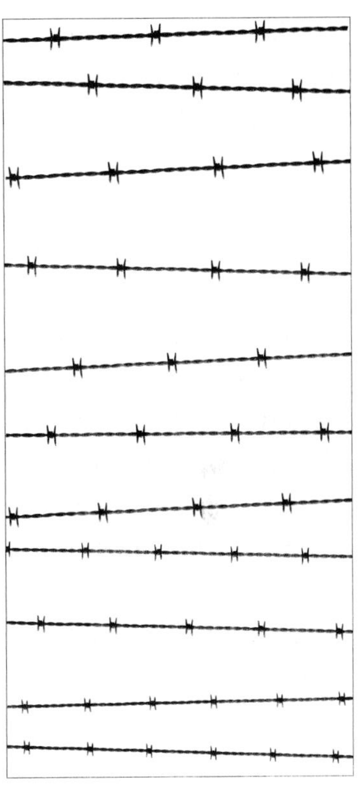

Ken used to listen intently to Oba-san's stories about World War II. Like many Japanese-Americans, she was taken from her home in San Francisco and sent to live in an **internment** camp in Utah. Ken knew that she had suffered when her rights as a citizen were taken away.

"There were deserts, mud, and snakes. Lots of barbed wire. We slept in crowded rooms," she recalled. "The washing rooms were filthy and it was freezing cold at night."

But the thing Ken's grandmother missed most at the camp was cooking. "We had no kitchens of our own. Everyone ate in a mess hall. We had to eat what we were given," she added, curling her lips in disgust. "I used to **fantasize** about making mochi—all kinds of mochi: raisin-cinnamon, sesame-garlic, cashew-date, but especially strawberry," Oba-san smiled in remembered delight.

Before the family was taken to the internment camp, she was just a little girl named Aiko. It was Aiko's job to **husk** the strawberries before her mother made them into Ichigo Daifuku, or strawberry sweet cakes. Her mother always called the treat "Aiko Cakes."

continued on next page

internment *adj.*, prison
fantasize *v.*, daydream
husk *v.*, remove the stem and leaves

Make Connections

5. Compare this story so far with other texts you have read about people's cultural heritage.

____

____

____

____

6. Why do you think a teenager would be interested in his grandparents' stories?

____

____

____

Make Connections, continued

A Sweet Tradition, continued

Now, in his own kitchen, Ken could still see his grandmother's graceful hands folding the edges of the dough. She had lovingly created good food, and she passed her **appreciation** on to him. He still loved to make the sweet strawberry cakes. Everyone seemed to value the care and attention it took to create the treat. Even his mother enjoyed them and teased him by calling them "Ken Cakes."

Ken loved American desserts, too. He enjoyed pumpkin pie and ice cream. He still ate his mother's chocolate chip cookies with milk. But his favorite was strawberry shortcake with whipped cream. There was just something about a strawberry...

Suddenly Ken felt a little foolish. He was standing in the middle of his kitchen holding a strawberry while he was miles away in his mind. Then he realized that the very best thing to do with a fresh strawberry was to just eat it with nothing else. He brought the strawberry to his mouth. He closed his eyes and **savored** the delicious fruit.

appreciation *n.,* understanding and enjoyment
savored *v.,* enjoyed

Make Connections

7. How is "A Sweet Tradition" like other stories you have read?

Sum It Up

8. What new ideas or information did you learn about the topic?

Self-Assessment

9. How did making connections help you get the most out of the story?

Name ______________________ Date ____________

Make Connections

Preview "Identity Through a Silent Language" so that you know what to expect when you read. As you read, make connections to ideas, other texts, and your own experiences.

Strategy at a Glance

Make Connections

When you make connections, you

- tap into what you already know about the topic and pay attention to what the selection reminds you of
- link what you're reading to your own experiences, things you know about the world, and other texts you've read.

DID YOU KNOW?

- Nearly 40,000 people in the U.S. younger than 18 are functionally deaf.
- 10,000 children in the U.S. have cochlear implants.

Identity Through a Silent Language

Imagine you can't hear. Would a device that could help you understand sound be a good idea? What if that device changed your culture and identity? Would you still choose it? That question is at the root of a heated **controversy**.

In the United States being deaf or hearing impaired qualifies as a disability. Yet for many deaf people, being deaf is much more than an inability to hear. The deaf have a rich culture, community, and language. Deafness is part of their identity.

Deaf teens have a strong sense of community.

continued on next page

controversy *n.*, debate

Make Connections

1. What is the topic of this passage? What do you know about the topic?

____

____

2. Is this passage fiction or nonfiction? How can you tell?

____

____

Make Connections, continued

Identity Through a Silent Language, continued

Technology can't make deaf persons hear, but it can help them process sounds. A doctor can **surgically** place a cochlear implant behind a deaf person's ear. This electronic device has a microphone. The microphone picks up sound. It turns the sound into electrical signals. Then it sends the signals to the **auditory** nerve.

The process is not an instant cure, however. First the patient recovers from the surgery. Then the implant is programmed. A technician works with the patient so that the implant sends signals at the right levels. This process can take weeks or even years. However, the implant allows many people to understand sounds in their environment. They can even enjoy a conversation in person or by telephone.

continued on next page

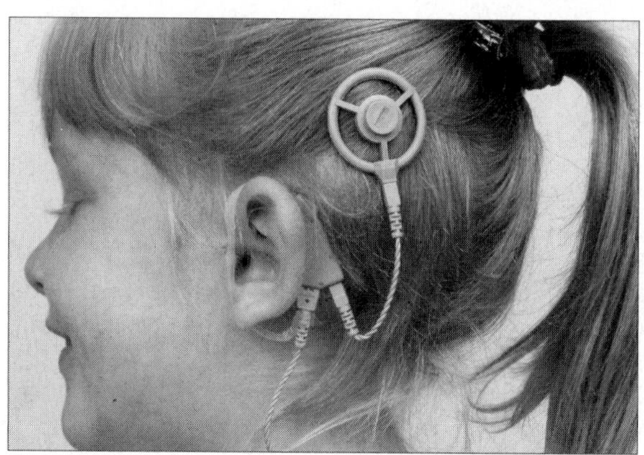

A cochlear implant

surgically *adv.,* through surgery
auditory *adj.,* related to hearing

Make Connections

3. What other text does this remind you of?

4. Technology can help deaf people process sounds. In what other ways does technology help people communicate?

Make Connections, continued

Identity Through a Silent Language, continued

Some members of the deaf community, however, consider the implants a threat. They do not view deafness as a disability. They believe that the deaf can function fully without speaking. They explain that the deaf community is a safe, tight-knit family of people. The deaf share a unique outlook on life. They worry that a child with a cochlear implant may feel **alienated** from both the hearing community and the deaf community.

"It is better to leave the child's sense of community firmly within the deaf community," they argue, "than to risk cutting the child off from the only community he or she has known."

continued on next page

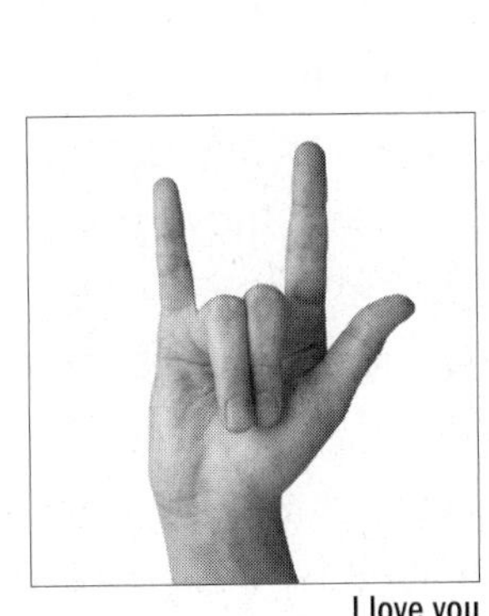

I love you

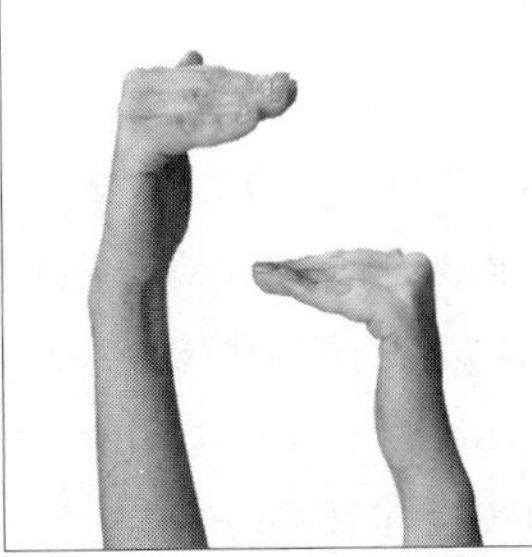

Hope

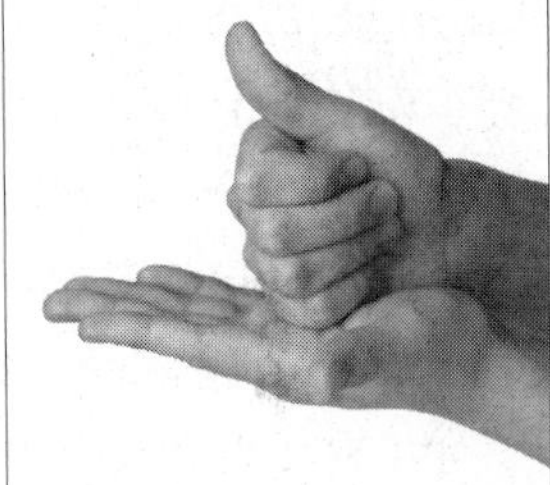

Help

Some American Sign Language (ASL) signs

alienated *adj.,* separated

Make Connections

5. Describe what community *you* feel most comfortable in.

6. Who do you think should decide whether a deaf child gets an implant or not? Explain.

Make Connections, continued

Identity Through a Silent Language, continued

Obviously, the debate over cochlear implants is **divisive**. Many see cochlear implants as a child's best chance at fitting in with the hearing world. Many hearing adults feel that opportunities for the deaf are limited unless they get the implants. Others point out that more and more organizations use sign language as part of their public presentations. This would suggest that there are more and more opportunities for deaf adults to work in **mainstream** jobs.

For deaf adults, cochlear implants are a matter of personal choice. How would you choose?

Students learning to be sign language interpreters

---

divisive *adj.,* causing conflict
mainstream *adj.,* the way the majority of people live

Make Connections

7. What did you know about the topic before you read "Identity Through a Silent Language?"

8. How do the issues and ideas in "Identity Through a Silent Language" connect to what you know about the world?

Self-Assessment

9. How did making connections help you understand the selection?

Name ______________________ Date ____________

Make Inferences About Characters

Preview the story so that you know what to expect when you read. As you read, underline what the main character says and does to help you make inferences about what she is thinking and feeling.

Strategy at a Glance

Make Inferences

To make inferences about characters, you

- think about situations you've been in that are similar to the ones in the story
- combine what you've read and what you know to figure out what makes the characters tick.

THE CHANCE FOR EXPRESSION

Janna answered the final test question and looked at the clock. Ten minutes left. She took out her sketch pad. At the top of the paper, Janna drew a sketch of Mr. Terence leaning on the corner of his desk. Then she covered the margins with sketches of the other students: Loc chewing on his pencil, Josie twirling her hair, Carlos staring out the window.

"Time's up," Mr. Terence finally said.

Janna picked up her backpack and dropped her test in the basket. Lunch period was next—Janna's favorite part of the day because she could draw without anyone interrupting her.

"Step aside, da Vinci!" Carlos bumped Janna on the way out the door. The basketball star, Carlos, had a nickname for everyone.

"Hope you don't shoot too many air balls tonight, Carlos," was Janna's snappy retort.

The next day, Mr. Terence called Janna up to his desk. "The school wants a mural celebrating all the championships our basketball team has won. Would you be interested?"

Janna played it cool, but secretly she was **ecstatic**. "Sure, Mr. T, if I can choose what I paint."

Three days later, she was sketching a cougar on the wall of the library building when Carlos walked by.

"Wow!" Carlos laughed, pointing to the sketch. "You're going to get busted for that graffiti."

Janna smiled. "Save your trash-talking for the court, Carlos."

"What's going up after the cougar?"

"You getting your shot blocked."

"Save your trash-talking for your paints, da Vinci." Carlos grinned.

Janna shook her head and began sketching the rest of the mural: Carlos hanging on the rim after jamming over their rivals, the Gators.

---

ecstatic *adj.*, extremely happy

Use the diagram to record your inferences about the main character.

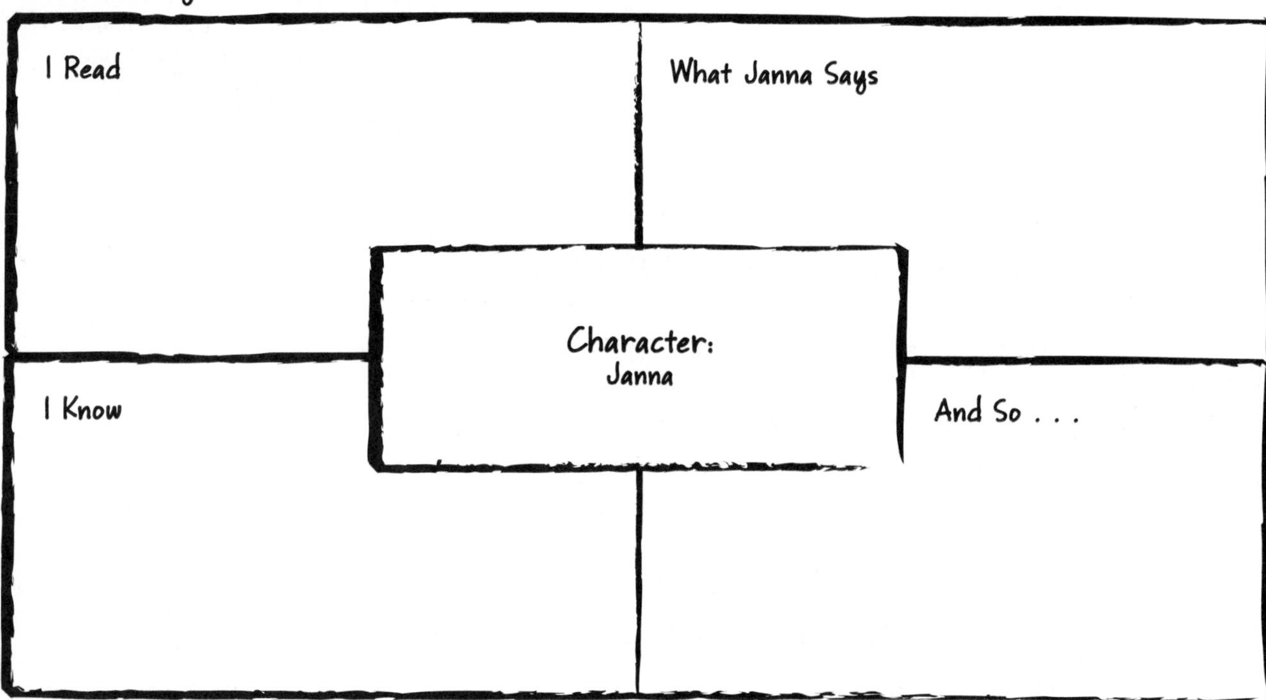

Talk About It

Tell your teacher or a classmate about a person you know who's similar to one of the characters in the story.

Make the Ideas Your Own

Why do you think Janna didn't show how happy she was to be asked to paint the mural? When have you been in a similar situation?

Name ______________________ Date __________

Make Inferences About the Theme

Preview the story so that you know what to expect when you read. As you read, underline important information to help you make inferences about the theme.

Strategy at a Glance

Make Inferences

When you make inferences about the theme, you

- look for characters' actions and story events that relate to big ideas and lessons about life
- ask yourself what you know that can help you understand the author's message
- put together what you know and details from the story.

What Friends Are For

"Why couldn't Stacy's parents have waited to move for another month?" Sean complained to D.J. "Nobody who's auditioned is half as good as she was."

The Battle of the Bands was in three weeks, and The Ragged Angels had practiced for it all year. With their lead singer gone, the Angels couldn't possibly win, especially with D.J. playing bass. D.J. was Sean's best friend, but he wasn't a very good bassist.

Sean's blindness never had limited his imagination. He had pictured the crowd screaming for his great band, until reality hit him. Without a singer, and with a clumsy bassist, the prospects did not look good.

Until Carla walked up to the microphone.

"Hi." Her voice was cool and breezy. "I'm Carla Brown." She blushed and stared at her feet.

"Glad you're here," said D.J. easily. "What do you want to sing?"

"D-do you know 'W-winter?'"

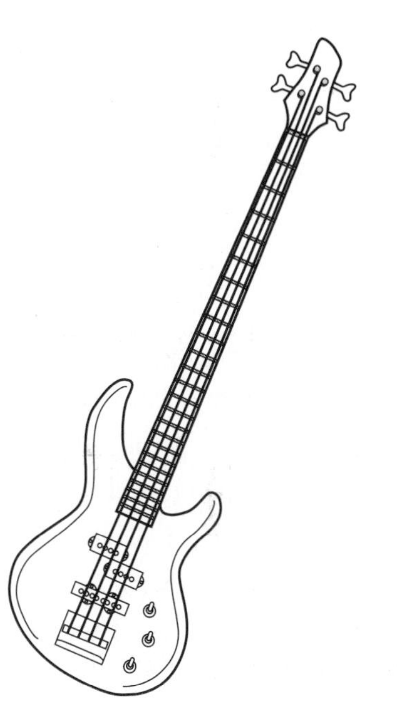

continued on next page

Use the inference chart to record the inferences you made in this part of the story.

I Read	I Know	And So . . .
		The theme is

As you read the rest of the story, continue underlining important information to help you make inferences about the theme.

What Friends Are For, continued

Jerry started drumming. Sean played the opening **riff**. D.J. established the bass line. Carla began singing. Sean stopped playing and stood **motionless**. Carla's voice was angelic.

"Gor-gee-ous!" breathed Jerry.

"Hey, guys," Sean said slowly. "We have a real shot at winning."

Carla looked up cautiously from behind her long auburn hair. "Does that mean I got the gig?"

"Certainly!" D.J. grinned.

The night of the Battle, Sean felt more nervous than ever. D.J. just wasn't picking it up. Sean was warming up when he heard it. Someone was playing slap bass. Really well. And it wasn't D.J. This bassist, whose name was Linus, might make Sean's dream come true, and he was willing to play that night. Sean's mind raced. He really wanted to win this contest and Linus could make the difference the band needed. He could just replace D.J. at the last moment…

Just then, the rest of the band walked in.

A long moment passed as D.J. stared at Linus in his place. "What's up?" he asked, perplexed.

"Sorry, D.J.," said Sean. "Linus was just filling in for my warm-up."

The Ragged Angels played their hearts out. When D.J. messed up the bridge, Sean soloed, and Carla sang over his bass line when he was out of key. They didn't win the trophy, but they had a great time trying.

---

riff *n.,* musical phrase
motionless *adj.,* without moving

Use the inference chart to record your inferences about the theme.

I Read	I Know	And So . . .
		The theme is

Name ____________________ Date __________

Make Inferences About Factual Information

Preview the passage so that you know what to expect when you read. As you read, underline the ideas the writer emphasizes.

Strategy at a Glance

Make Inferences

To make inferences in nonfiction, you

- pay attention to what the author emphasizes about the topic and how it is presented
- think about what you already know about the topic
- combine what the author says with what you know to get the unstated meanings.

DID YOU KNOW?

- The United States generates more than 200 million tons of trash every year.
- Recycling is one way to cut down on landfill.

Recycled Self-Expression

Finding Art

Bobby Hansson began making art, jewelry, and musical instruments from found objects in 1955. He didn't want to use expensive craft supplies for his artwork. He started using **discarded** items because they were free. His creative eye was actually drawn to things that had a one-way ticket to the junkyard. Empty TV dinner trays, bent license plates, and old wires had served their purpose. In Hansson's imagination, they became decorative and useful objects. One of his first unique creations grew out of a plastic toy boot, a turkey baster, and a straw. It became the Shoe Horn, a musical instrument.

Hansson turned found objects into art.

continued on next page

discarded *adj.*, thrown out

Use the inference chart to record the inferences you made in this part of the article.

I Read	I Know	And So . . .

As you read the rest of the article, continue underlining the ideas the writer emphasizes.

Recycled Self-Expression, continued

New Music

Hansson attended a performance of the Juilliard String Quartet in 1956. It struck him as an opportunity to develop his craft in new ways. He decided to create the Junkyard String Quartet. That musical group has now **expanded** to become the 47-piece Junkyard Orchestra. All the sections of a typical orchestra are represented. The Junkyard Orchestra has woodwinds, horns, strings, and percussion. As you'd expect, the instruments do not look typical. The flute was once a tomato paste can. What do you think the Canjo started out as? Here's a hint. A player strums it like a banjo. A lawn mower handle and a maple syrup bucket become a bass guitar.

Hansson plays his "Tin Horn."

Sharing the Joy of Junk

Hansson's art has left its junkyard **status** behind. His creations are regarded as works of art. In 2002, The Noyes Museum of Art in New Jersey displayed instruments from the Junkyard Orchestra. Now, museums across the country have shown Hansson's works.

---

expanded *v.,* grown in size
status *n.,* position

Use the chart to record your inferences.

I Read	I Know	And So . . .

Make the Ideas Your Own

What are some ways that you can cut down on the amount of trash you create? Are there ways you could recycle things?

Name ____________________ Date __________

Make Inferences About the Poet's Message

Preview the poem so that you know what to expect when you read. Then read the poem once for enjoyment.

Strategy at a Glance

Make Inferences

To make inferences about poetry, you

- notice words that appeal to your senses or that repeat
- connect the poet's descriptions to your own experience
- combine what the poet tells you with your experience and feelings to understand the poet's message.

Read the poem a few more times. As you read, circle words that help you create pictures in your mind.

1. My Mental Pictures:

____

____

____

____

____

2. More Mental Pictures:

____

____

____

____

3. My Connections:

____

____

____

____

Wild Land Cook

—Hillary Ostermiller

I cook this meal
over small sage flames
camped far away from roads.
Sizzling in a cast-iron **skillet**,
searing flavors, sealing my past
on this wild land.

I taste west-traveled earth
not fumes nor fast foods,
but dirt from dust-cut winds
blown in this kitchen under stars.
I taste the flavor of history.

I cook this meal,
marinated in America's past.
Jack rabbits, cattle, and bison
rubbed with train cars, stockyards,
black pepper, tractor-pull of barley,
cooked over plaid work shirts, rodeos,
snap-buttons, hard leather boots.

A meal marinated in frontiers,
rubbed with hand-sewn apron, salt,
soft braids, star-punctured nights,
cooked over mesquite smoke, native lands
stretched like hides, borders busting at the seams.

continued on next page

skillet *n.*, frying pan
searing *v.*, burning the surface slightly

Use the chart below the passage to record your inferences about the poet's message.

Talk About It

Compare your chart to a classmate's. Did you take away the same message?

Make the Ideas Your Own

In what ways do you feel "the flavor of history?" Give specific examples.

Wild Land Cook, continued

I eat this meal of memory,
camped far away from the road,
robust chew,
rich taste of history.
America's past now present taste broadens
as stories fill the air.

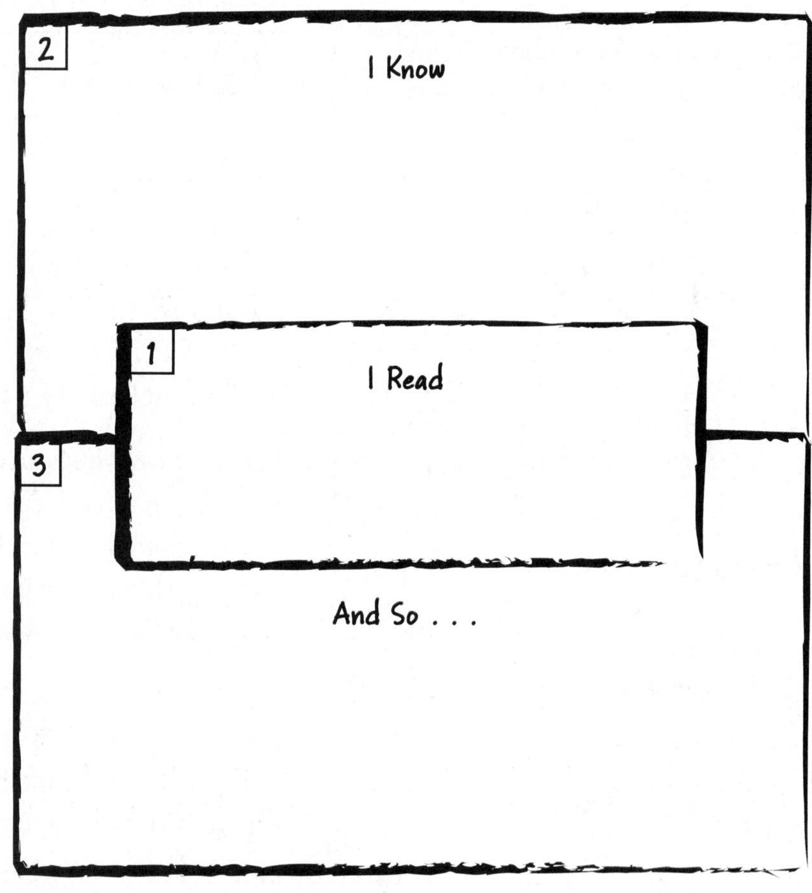

Name ______________________ Date ____________

Make Inferences

Preview the story so that you know what to expect when you read. As you read, underline important ideas and information in the text to help you understand the characters and theme.

Strategy at a Glance

Make Inferences

When you make inferences in fiction, you

- think about what you already know about ideas and information in the text
- combine what you read with what you know to figure out what the author does not say directly.

Taping the Truth

"Sophomore Sayoko Murai's first film is **earnest,** direct, and surprisingly beautiful. This is a student with a real gift. Watch out, Steven Spielberg."

I read the glowing review of my first movie with disbelief. I was too worried about the **controversy** that my film had caused to take in the praise. I never meant to be the center of a debate. I just wanted to make a movie.

It all started when I wanted to film real students in class. "Don't even think about videotaping in algebra," Ms. Fenmoore warned.

I met with similar responses in other classes. Most teachers didn't want their classes disrupted. Students, of course, were eager to be in my film. Too eager, in fact. They all wanted to be stars. It was difficult to shoot them in natural situations.

continued on next page

---

earnest *adj.,* eager and serious
controversy *n.,* debate

Check Your Understanding

1. Reread the film review in the first paragraph. Restate it in your own words.

____

____

2. What are the important ideas in this part of the story?

____

____

____

Make Inferences, continued

Taping the Truth, continued

So I changed my focus from students to things. The rusty pipe dripping orange water in the bathroom. Broken windows in the gym. Layers of dust in the basement classroom that gave students hacking coughs. I thought I was aware of all the problems before, but the evidence I found surprised even me. I didn't know a lot about health issues, but I did know when I saw situations that cried out for attention.

I knew, however, that I didn't want to just show a series of ugly images. I wanted to **convey** a sense of mission, a feeling of purpose. I wanted to draw my viewers into the scenes as if they lived there day to day, as we students did. I wanted to tap into their pride in our school and see how some situations damaged our **reputation**.

What would be the best approach? I wanted to be a filmmaker and not just a kid with a camera.

continued on next page

---

convey *v.*, communicate
reputation *n.*, what people thought of us

Make Inferences

3. Why do you think Sayoko's film caused controversy?

4. What does Sayoko mean by "I wanted to be a filmmaker and not just a kid with a camera"?

Make Inferences, continued

Taping the Truth, continued

My favorite film director says the best filmmakers can make an ugly scene look beautiful and a beautiful scene look ugly. Could I do that with my film? I tried shooting the same object from different angles and in different lights. I swore a couple of students to secrecy and had them give the **impressions** each shot gave them. Then I chose the ones that seemed to give the impression I wanted.

I decided to use only very subtle background music. There would be no narration and no captions for the pictures. I wanted the images to speak for themselves.

When the film was finished, I showed it to my dad. Two weeks later, he **screened** it at a meeting of the Evergreen Parents Club. Lakeesha Hart, a local reporter, was at the meeting. That night, Hart kicked off her five-part newspaper series on the poor conditions at Evergreen High!

The next thing I knew, the School Board was involved. They heard about the film from the Parents Club and requested a showing at their next meeting. I had no way of knowing whether this was a good or a bad thing. I wasn't going to hide my work, though. So I gave the Superintendent's Office a copy of my film and waited to see how much trouble I had gotten myself into.

continued on next page

---

impressions *n.,* feelings, responses
screened *v.,* showed

Stop and Think

5. How do you know that the film has a powerful effect on the community?

6. What would Sayoko do if her film did get her "in trouble?" What makes you think this?

Make Inferences, continued

Taping the Truth, continued

I could tell that Superintendent Owens had never watched my film, but he was quick to **denounce** it. "This film exaggerates the situation. Our schools are in excellent shape. We have no **funds** for repairs," he argued.

Other staff members joined the debate, and the **hype** didn't end until the Board finally got to see my film. I was invited to sit in the Board Room as the Board Members and the public watched. Afterward, the audience sat in stunned silence. Finally, the Chairwoman said, "Sayoko Murai's film is convincing. It's time for major improvements."

The Board voted that evening to allocate more funds to the Building Maintenance Fund. I began seeing repair crews working on sore spots around Evergreen High School within a week.

I admit that my skin feels prickly when I see my film's effect on my community. Since then, my eyes are like the lens of a camera. My next idea is pushing me to pick up the camera, and I can't wait to see what happens.

---

denounce *v.*, speak against
funds *n.*, money
hype *n.*, public excitement

Make Inferences

7. What did you already know about the ideas in the story before you read "Taping the Truth"?

8. Combine what you know with information about the events and characters. What is the author's message?

Self-Assessment

9. How did making inferences help you get the most out of the story?

Name ______________________ Date ____________

Make Inferences

Preview the passage so that you know what to expect when you read. As you read, underline ideas and information in the text.

Strategy at a Glance

Make Inferences

When you make inferences in nonfiction, you

- think about what you already know about ideas and information in the text
- combine what you read with what you know to figure out the author's full meaning.

DID YOU KNOW?

- Pablo Picasso was a world-famous Spanish painter of the 20th century.
- Dragons are part of Chinese New Year festivals.

SIDEWALK ART IN 3D

Pavement Picasso

In Britain, some sidewalk drawings now have a whole new **dimension**. They appear in three dimensions, or 3D. The creator of these works, Julian Beever, is known as the "Pavement Picasso." People don't have to go to a gallery to see his work. Ordinary pedestrians just look down near their feet to appreciate his talent.

Beever's sidewalk creations include unique advertisements, cartoons, and reproductions of famous portraits. They appear so lifelike that walkers hesitate when they walk past them. These **optical illusions** have won Beever worldwide fame.

A sidewalk optical illusion

continued on next page

dimension *n.*, aspect or nature
optical illusions *n.*, tricks of the eye

Make Inferences

1. Why do you think Julian Beever is called the "Pavement Picasso"?

____

____

2. Why do people hesitate when they walk past Beever's work?

____

____

Make Inferences, continued

Sidewalk Art in 3D, continued

Creating Tricks of the Eye

Beever **distorts** images to trick the viewer's eye. From a certain angle, objects appear to jump out of or sink into the pavement or sidewalk. It looks as though you might fall into his swimming pools and manholes. You feel you might **collide** with umbrellas, or trip over computers in your path.

Beever's interest in this technique began when he was working in Brussels, Belgium. He discovered the works of artists who were able to create the appearance of depth. He **imitated** their technique using chalk. Beever experimented with a variety of projects. Finally, he could create chalk drawings that appeared to reach into the sky and dig deep into the earth.

continued on next page

Beever uses chalk to create 3D images.

distorts *v.,* changes, twists
collide *v.,* crash
imitated *v.,* copied

Check Your Understanding

3. What does the author want you to know about Beever's art?

4. How did Beever learn to do this type of painting?

Make Inferences, continued

Sidewalk Art in 3D, continued

How does he create the 3D effect in his art? Beever sets up a camera on a **tripod**. He keeps the camera in one spot and checks every mark he makes. "It's really just playing with perspective to make it appear different from what it really is," Beever says. He even invites onlookers to view his work through the camera's lens.

A Cat in Dragon's Clothing

In January 2006, Beever used his talents for a Chinese New Year celebration in Birmingham, England. His **elaborate** plan had a touch of humor. Beever spent three days sketching a Chinese dragon onto the streets in Chinatown. According to the Chinese calendar, 2006 was the year of the dog. In fun, Beever drew a cat in a dragon costume.

continued on next page

---

tripod *n.,* three-legged stand
elaborate *adj.,* detailed

Make Inferences

5. What do you think Beever is trying to achieve with his work?

____

____

____

____

Visualize

6. Imagine Beever working on his art. Describe the scene.

____

____

____

____

____

____

Make Inferences, continued

Sidewalk Art in 3D, continued

Art for Everybody

For each of his drawings, Beever bends over the sidewalk in heat and cold for up to three days. "It's very physically **demanding** to do it," the artist admits. "I have a stool which I lie on which removes some of the physical stress."

Beever's sidewalk drawings are created in chalk. So they last only as long as the weather allows. Once it rains, they're gone. Some people even consider the work graffiti. They say it doesn't belong on public streets. To Beever, however, "Art shouldn't be locked away in galleries and libraries and books. Art should be for everybody."

Beever works on a chalk art masterpiece

demanding *adj.,* difficult, stressful

Make Inferences

7. What did you already know about the ideas in the article before you read "Sidewalk Art in 3D"?

8. Combine what you know with the information about Julian Beever's artwork. What is the author's message?

Self-Assessment

9. How did making inferences help you figure out the author's full meaning?

Name ______________________ Date ____________

Form Generalizations

Preview "...And Justice for All" so that you know what to expect when you read. As you read, underline the important ideas.

Strategy at a Glance

Synthesize

To form generalizations, you

- focus on ideas the writer emphasizes and that you think are important
- think about how the important ideas fit with one another and with what you know
- create a broad statement that covers many of the examples presented in the text.

DID YOU KNOW?

- In the 1800s, several families often lived in one filthy, rundown apartment in a tenement building.
- Children as young as 8 years old had to work.

... And Justice for All

During the Industrial Revolution in the 19th Century, thousands of Americans moved from farms to cities. Their lives changed dramatically. Steam-powered ships, railways, and electric power generators saved time and increased production in factories. But rapid progress in industry had an ugly side, too. Workers **toiled** at dangerous jobs in crowded factories and mills. They often worked as much as 16 hours a day. They earned little pay.

In the 20th century, workers began protesting unsafe working conditions. They spoke out against unfair employment practices. They fought for 8-hour workdays, minimum wages, and 2-day weekends. Thus the labor movement was born. It won **benefits** that are common in today's society. Organized labor also helped to pass the Civil Rights Act of 1964. Companies could no longer refuse to hire workers because of skin color, race, religion, sex, or nationality.

Workers protesting working conditions in 1937

toiled *v.*, worked hard

benefits *n.*, things a company gives its workers, such as paid vacation and health insurance

1. How do the ideas in the selection fit together?

____

____

Preview "Photographer of the Dark Side" so that you know what to expect when you read. As you read, underline the important ideas.

Photographer of the Dark Side

In the late 1800s many poor Americans lived and worked in **unsanitary** and overcrowded conditions. Concerned social activists and journalists began **investigating** these situations. Jacob Riis was one of those journalists. He took his camera into the tenements where poor workers lived. His book, *How the Other Half Lives,* showed the misery of families in New York City's slums. Wealthy and middle-class citizens who read the book were shocked.

Jacob Riis's photos of homeless children shocked most Americans.

Riis's photos soon led the way to better housing. The city took action. It passed the Tenement House Act in 1901. Run-down tenements were improved and new housing was constructed. Riis's photos also gave America a unique record of its workers during a time of great change.

unsanitary *adj.,* unclean and unhealthy
investigating *v.,* studying, researching

2. Record the important ideas from each selection. Then put the ideas together and write a generalization.

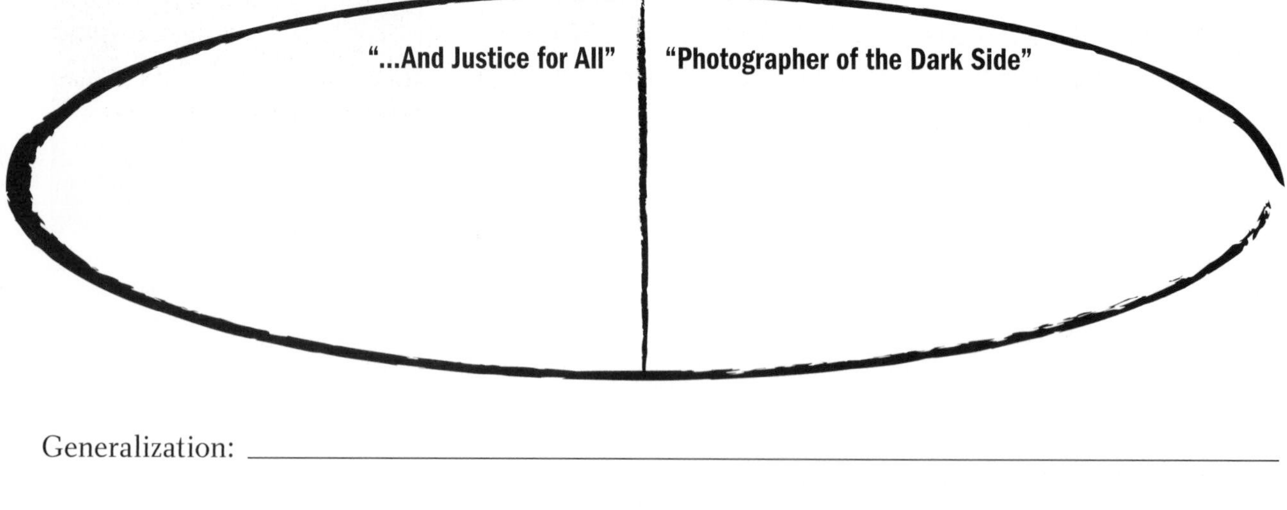

Generalization: ______________________________

Name ______________________ Date __________

Draw Conclusions: From a Single Text

Preview the article so that you know what to expect when you read. As you read, underline what you think is noteworthy.

Strategy at a Glance

Synthesize

To draw conclusions, you

- pay attention to what the writer emphasises
- think about how the ideas go together
- decide what to think.

DID YOU KNOW?

- A microchip is a tiny slice of material that makes electronic connections.
- A microchip can be implanted to help you find a lost pet.

Microchip Controversy

Librarians around the world are raving about a tiny square tag that promises to transform their work. The tiny chips are attached to books, DVDs, and CDs. These microchips send radio signals containing information about the item.

Good-by, Barcodes!

With this new technology, librarians no longer need to scan barcodes. Patrons **bypass** long checkout lines. They can wave their books in the direction of a chip reader and head out the door. Librarians can check in an entire stack of materials with a wave of a wand.

Privacy Problems?

New technology is not always used the way its creators intended. People will discover other uses for it. As you walk along carrying your library book, it emits a radio signal. The signal can be picked up from **remote** sites. Is this new technology chipping away at your right to privacy?

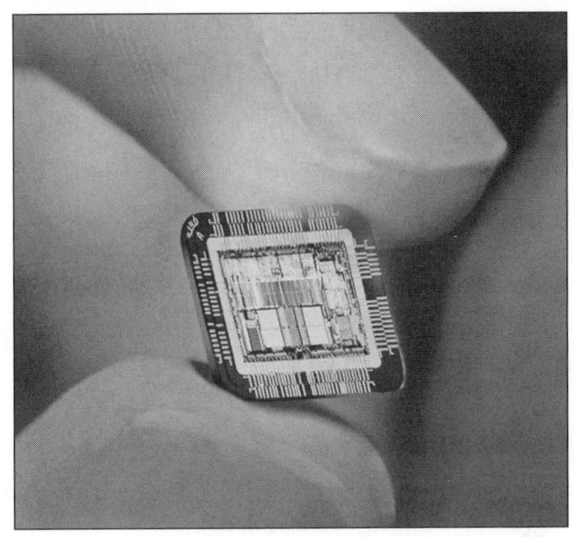

The small size of a microchip makes it very useful.

---

bypass *v.*, avoid
remote *adj.*, far away

1. Given all the information, what do you think about libraries using microchips? Be sure to explain your answer.

____

____

____

Draw Conclusions: From Multiple Texts

Preview "Freedom to Read" so that you know what to expect when you read. As you read, underline what you think is noteworthy.

DID YOU KNOW?

- The U.S. Constitution forbids restrictions on freedom of speech, with a few exceptions.
- Some libraries ban books for obscenity or profanity.

FREEDOM TO READ

Alyssa Leigh was a freedom fighter in the war on censorship. While other communities demanded that controversial books be **banned**, Leigh fought to keep them on the library's shelves. As a librarian, she believed that residents of her small Kansas town had the right to read whatever they choose.

In 1961, the Central City High School district banned Henry Miller's *Tropic of Cancer.* In an act of **dissent**, Leigh stored copies of the book in her desk. She loaned them to anyone who was interested. She fought through protests, rallies, and petitions. After a year, *Tropic of Cancer* was back in circulation. Leigh had won.

Fierce opposition continued when other books were banned. But Leigh never stopped voicing her opinion. Throughout her forty-year career, the library remained a beacon for freedom of expression.

---

banned *adj.,* kept away from the public
dissent *v.,* disagreement

2. Use the synthesis chart to pause and reflect on the new information.

TOPIC: Privacy and Library Use

Selection	What Are the Issues?
"Microchip Controversy"	
"Freedom to Read"	

Sample Conclusion: ______________________________

____

____

Name ______________________ Date ____________

Compare and Contrast Ideas

Preview the texts so that you know what to expect when you read. Underline important ideas in each text.

Strategy at a Glance

Synthesize

To compare and contrast ideas, you

- focus on important ideas in each text
- identify what writers or sources agree on and specific examples of how they disagree
- organize your findings in a diagram and sum up the ideas.

A New Rainbow

—Lorraine McCombs

I hear voices laughing outside, see my best
friends' eyes. Brown, green.
Blue, black. **Peering** in the window at my
Grandma and me.

Was a time, my Grandma says, when your
friends looked only like you:
Brown, tan, black. Sometimes reddish-
brown or yellow-brown.
But always black, always just like you.
Colors in the chocolate rainbow.

Color mattered then, Grandma says. Does
it matter now?
Grandma smiles and waves a **gnarled**
brown hand at me.
I turn and wave back as I add my color to
the new rainbow.

---

peering *v.,* looking
gnarled *adj.,* twisted

Our Pain, Our Progress

—Karl Williams

It took twelve stitches to close up my soccer injury. When granddad came in to see how I was doing, he showed me a scar I never knew he had. When I asked about it, he sighed and began to speak almost **inaudibly**.

"It was my sixteenth birthday, August 28, 1963," he said. "I decided it was time I started acting like a man, so I stood up and marched for our future. For our freedom. They turned the dogs on us. The pain was incredible, but that bite helped set us free."

Then he looked proudly at a photo of my soccer team. We stood together—white, black, Asian, Hispanic—as teammates. "Now, your scar will remind us of how far we've come," he said.

---

inaudibly *adv.,* silently

Now organize your findings about the two selections in a diagram.

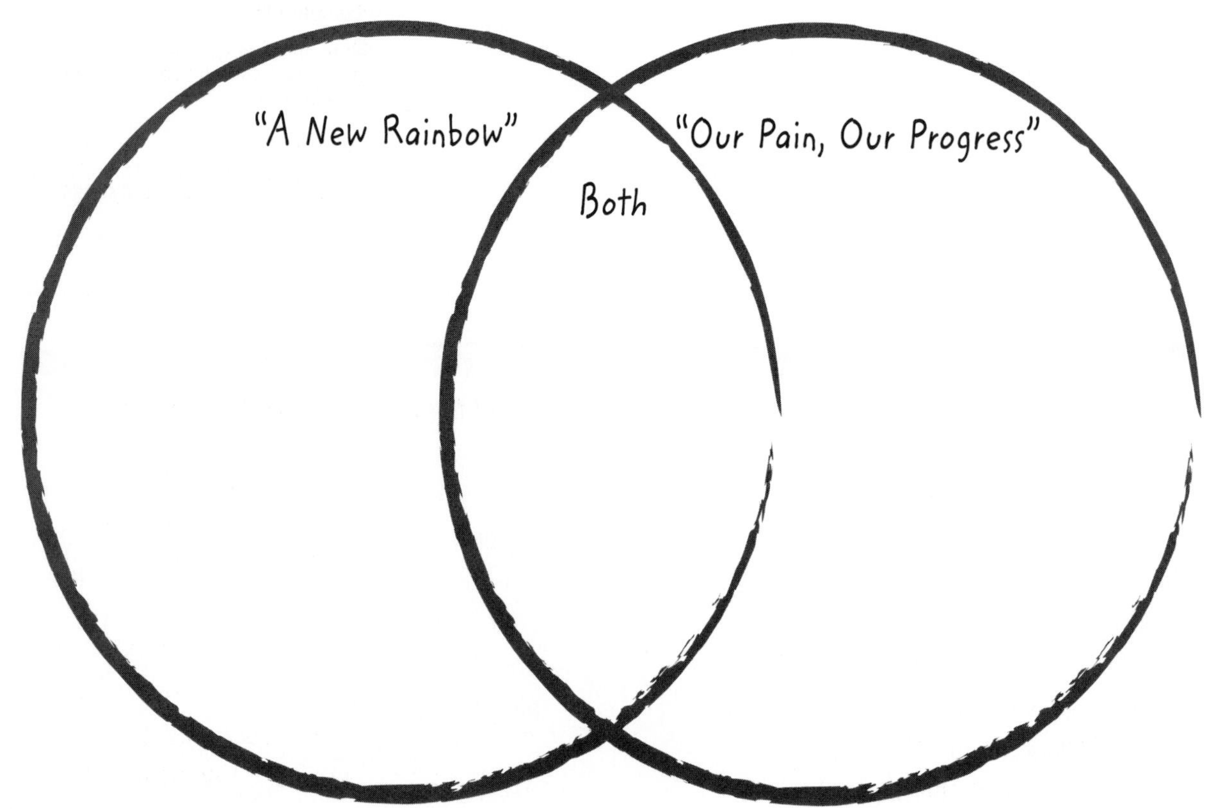

Use your completed diagram to compare and contrast the ideas. Write your conclusions or new opinion.

____

____

____

____

____

____

Talk About It

Tell your teacher or a classmate your conclusions.

Make the Ideas Your Own

What did you learn about race relations from reading the selections?

____

____

____

Name ______________________ Date __________

Take a Position

Preview the texts so that you know what to expect when you read. Underline important ideas in each text.

Strategy at a Glance

Synthesize

When you take a position, you

- think about facts, opinions, and arguments you already know about the question
- gather information from several texts and think about how much evidence there is for or against each position
- use information that is important to you to take a position.

Tolerance Is on the Menu

As students left the cafeteria last night, it was clear that the multicultural potluck was a huge success. Everyone enjoyed the event. There were foods from Poland, India, Mexico, and all the other ethnicities of our student body. But most importantly, all students mixed together **casually**. This was not the usual cafeteria scene where **cliques** of students group themselves by ethnicity.

So why let the potluck's success stop with a one-night event? A tasty dish is a combination of many different ingredients. But you have to put them all together. Assigned cafeteria seats is the recipe students need. Then they'll learn **tolerance** toward each other. Everyone has something to offer. The more we learn about others, the more likely we are to respect differences.

---

casually *adv.,* easily, informally
cliques *n.,* groups that keep others out
tolerance *n.,* an accepting attitude

Letter to the Editor

Dear South High Administration,

It happened again today. I showed up at my assigned seat in the cafeteria, **gobbled** down my lunch in silence, and left without saying a thing. The cafeteria is now more like the library—quiet and an unpopular place to be. I sit in classes all day. Only at lunch do I get to relax. I want to talk with my friends during lunch, not be forced to sit by people I don't know.

It's that new rule. All students are told where to sit. Whose idea was it to force ethnic groups to mix socially? Being forced to hang with kids I don't know is making me **resent** them. Forcing groups to mix actually causes **frictions** that didn't exist before! Please consider changing the rule.

Shavonda Walker, Junior

---

gobbled *v.,* quickly ate
resent *v.,* dislike
frictions *n.,* problems between groups

Take a Position, continued

Now organize your findings about the issue in a Pro/Con chart.

ISSUE: Ethnic Groups Mixing Together

Pro	Con

Review the information in your chart. Write your position:

____

____

Talk About It

Tell your teacher or a classmate your position on the issue.

Make the Ideas Your Own

How has this article changed your thinking? What do you know now about tolerance and ethnic cliques?

____

____

____

____

Synthesize

Preview the text so that you know what to expect when you read.

Read and synthesize the story. As you read, underline important ideas in the text and take notes about how the ideas fit together.

Strategy at a Glance

Synthesize

When you synthesize, you

- figure out how the important ideas fit together in a way that you haven't thought of before
- take a position on the writer's ideas and opinions about the topic.

A Jacket, a Quilt—a Dilemma

Today, Liz was on a mission. She was preparing for her senior year spring break trip. She hung her new snowboarding jacket proudly on her door. It was her first purchase with the money she'd saved over the past four years.

"Tornado Alley Aid called," Liz's mom said. "A tornado hit Woodhill. I wonder how Lance came out of this. The group is headed down there next week to help."

"But next week is spring break!" Liz burst out. She began throwing things toward the bag she planned to take on her trip. The excitement of the snowboarding trip seemed to have **morphed** into rage. What did that mean?

As objects continued to fly across the room, one scarf seemed to hang in midair. As Liz lifted the scarf she realized it was caught on a nail that held a beautiful quilt to the wall.

continued on next page

morphed *v.*, changed

Synthesize

1. What are the important ideas in this section of the story?

____

____

____

2. What kind of person is Liz? How do you know?

____

____

Synthesize, continued

A Jacket, a Quilt—a Dilemma, continued

This was not an ordinary quilt. For Liz, it had meaning far beyond its detailed patterns. She thought back to the day the quilt became hers.

Liz had joined a group organized by Tornado Alley Aid. They had gone to help in Woodhill, a town right along the path of powerful tornadoes. They had had a mission then, too. They were going to rebuild homes, and Lance's home was one of them. It felt good to be doing something that really helped the victims. It also felt good to be away from home on her own.

Then everything changed. On the second day in Woodhill, Liz was hammering roofing onto Lance's house when Barry, the group leader, **drew** her aside.

"You need to call home," he said. "Your mom has been in a car accident. She is in **critical** condition."

Suddenly being away from home seemed lonely instead of exciting. The people in Woodhill needed Liz, but picturing her mother lying in a hospital bed, Liz knew she would want Liz to be with her.

continued on next page

drew *v.*, took
critical *adj.*, serious

Synthesize

3. What events caused Liz to travel to Woodhill?

4. Twice the author writes that Liz was "on a mission." Compare and contrast the two situations.

Synthesize, continued

A Jacket, a Quilt—a Dilemma, continued

It was Lance's comment that helped Liz make up her mind.

"Your mom needs you now," he said. "There will still be work in Tornado Alley after your mom recovers."

Frightened, Liz managed to get a ticket for a bus that would get her home. But she **insisted on** saying good-bye to her fellow volunteers at the work site before she left. After all the hugs, Lance stepped forward.

"Here," Lance said, as he wrapped a quilt over Liz's **quivering** shoulders. "Now, go take care of your mom."

All the way home on the bus, Liz huddled under that quilt whenever the fears about her mom seemed too much to bear.

When she finally reached the hospital, Liz was relieved to find that her mother was out of danger and would have only a few scars to remind her of the **ordeal**. As Liz sat beside her mother's bed, she began to study the quilt she had worn all the way home. It was then that she realized what Lance had done. He'd given her his mother's quilt, one of the few treasures left from his destroyed home.

continued on next page

insisted on *v.,* made sure
quivering *v.,* shaking
ordeal *n.,* difficult time

Synthesize

5. What do Lance's actions tell you about his character?

___

___

6. Think about how Lance and Liz react in different situations. What do you think the author is saying about human nature? Do you agree?

___

___

___

___

Synthesize, continued

A Jacket, a Quilt—a Dilemma, continued

Now, that patched quilt decorated a wall in Liz's room, and Lance's community had been hit again. Liz touched the red jacket, and then glanced at her mom. She could still see a scar that began above her mom's left eyebrow and faded into her hairline. Her mom was safe now and Liz had worked hard to save money for the snowboarding trip. Surely she deserved a treat. There were a lot of Tornado Alley volunteers. They could take care of Woodhill this time.

Then Liz's hand moved to the quilt. Lance had been kind to her at a time when he had troubles of his own. His selfless action had made a huge difference in Liz's life. How could she take off on a pleasure trip when people in Woodhill were suffering again?

Liz reached up and took the quilt off the wall. "It's time to return Lance's quilt," she said.

Synthesize

7. Synthesize "A Jacket, a Quilt—a Dilemma." What was Liz's dilemma in this story? Use information from different parts of the story in your answer.

8. Was it easy or difficult for Liz to make the decision? Write your opinion about how Liz resolved her dilemma.

Self-Assessment

9. How did synthesizing ideas from different parts of the story help you form your own ideas?

Name ______________________ Date ____________

Synthesize

Preview the text so that you know what to expect when you read.

Read and synthesize the article. As you read, underline important ideas in the text and take notes about how the ideas fit together.

Strategy at a Glance

Synthesize

When you synthesize, you

- figure out how the important ideas fit together in a way that you haven't thought of before
- take a position on the writer's ideas and opinions about the topic.

DID YOU KNOW?

- A curfew is a law that says that certain persons must be inside their homes at specific times.

Home by Ten: The Teenage Curfew Debate

Curfews for Young Adults

What is your community like at night? Are you allowed to go out alone to a youth center? Can you meet your friends in the park? Many teenagers enjoy going out at night to have fun.

But teens also take on responsibility. Young adults drive cars and hold jobs. They participate in sports and clubs. These activities sometimes occur when city curfews say teens must be off the streets.

continued on next page

Communities often post curfew hours.

Synthesize

1. According to this author, what are reasons that teens are out at night? For what other reasons might teens go out at night?

____

____

____

2. How might city curfews interfere with teenage responsibilities?

____

____

____

____

____

Synthesize, continued

Home by Ten: The Teenage Curfew Debate, continued

Laws that prevent teenagers from being away from home at night are not new. **Juvenile** curfews have existed in American cities since the 1890s. Curfews **dictate** when teens must be home. Some cities allow **exceptions** to the curfew rules.

The Pros and Cons

Not everyone agrees that curfews are useful. Some argue that teens learn self-discipline by setting their own schedule. Others say, "Let them set their own schedules during the daytime. At night they should follow the community's schedule." Many feel that parents should take some responsibility for teens' whereabouts at night.

continued on next page

Police monitor curfew violations.

juvenile *n.,* youth
dictate *v.,* state
exceptions *n.,* situations where the rule doesn't apply

Synthesize

3. What is the main idea of the first paragraph? Write it in your own words.

____

____

____

4. Why do some people oppose curfews? Write their reasons in your own words.

____

____

____

____

____

Synthesize, continued

Home by Ten: The Teenage Curfew Debate, continued

Councilwoman Diane Holland supports the curfew law in her town of Tomball City, Texas. She explains that it "helps preserve the peace and makes it safer for businesses and juveniles." City officials work to make their cities as safe as possible. Teens, as part of the community, need protection as well. In addition, many cities establish curfews to cut down on teenage crime.

Critics assert that curfews limit personal freedom. The Constitution gives citizens the right to peacefully **assemble.** People have challenged curfew laws based on teens' constitutional rights. They **contend** that curfews unfairly punish teenagers who have evening activities.

continued on next page

Many juvenile curfews go into effect at 10 P.M.

---

assemble *v.,* come together
contend *v.,* say, argue

Check Your Understanding

5. Who do city officials say benefits from curfew laws?

6. Why do some people believe that curfew laws violate teens' constitutional rights?

Synthesize, continued

Home by Ten: The Teenage Curfew Debate, continued

The Solution

The debate could be settled if research proved that curfews really reduce teenage crime. At this time, no clear evidence supports that. Statistics show that juvenile crime does not **peak** during curfew hours. Teenage crime is highest during daylight hours.

Officials continuously research ways to keep all citizens, including teens, safe both day and night. If curfews don't protect people, another solution might be needed.

One thing is clear. Communities want to protect all their citizens, so the debate over curfews will continue.

A downtown street during curfew hours

peak *v.,* reach their highest point

Synthesize

7. Synthesize the article. Find two ideas that struck you and put them together. Write about a new realization you have.

8. What is your position on juvenile curfews? Use important information from the article to support your position.

Self-Assessment

9. How did synthesizing information help you take a position on the topic of juvenile curfews?

Name ______________________ Date ____________

Fiction: What's Your Strategy?

Use strategies while you read "Golden Chances."

Be a Strategic Reader

When you are a strategic reader, you
- know the strategies in your toolbox
- choose strategies that work for the text that you're reading
- are flexible—switch or add strategies as you need to.

DID YOU KNOW?
- People who are often late actually dislike the habit.
- Some schools offer time management workshops for students who are frequently tardy.

Before you read, choose a strategy from the *Strategy Toolbox* on page 174.

1. The type of text I will read:

____

____

____

____

As you read, make sure the strategy you chose works for you:

2. How I make the strategy work:

____

____

____

____

____

3. Another strategy I used:

____

____

____

____

____

GOLDEN CHANCES

Ray's lungs burned as he sprinted down the hallway. When he finally burst into Mrs. Garcia's American History class, everyone looked up. The teacher pointed a piece of chalk at him.

"Ray! Late again, I see."

"I'm sorry," Ray murmured.

"Please find your seat. And I'd like a word with you after class," Mrs. Garcia warned, crossing her arms. Ray's habit of being late was always getting him into trouble. It was hopeless.

Ray listened attentively as Mrs. Garcia pointed to a poster of the first **transcontinental** railroad. "Railroads helped open up the West to **commerce** and industry," the teacher said. Ray's thoughts began to stray. He had been racing for a train last Saturday night. He had missed the train and the concert. What a disappointment!

Now Mrs. Garcia was holding up a book. "You will write an essay on *The Grapes of Wrath* in two weeks." Ray groaned. He didn't mind reading. But grapes were the reason Ray was late this morning. Grape *juice,* to be exact. He had spilled a glass of it all over his white shirt at breakfast. By the time he had found a clean shirt, the bus was long gone.

"Ray!" Ray snapped out of his daydream.

"What can you tell us about the first pioneers to reach California during the Gold Rush?" Mrs. Garcia asked.

"G-g-old Rush?" he stuttered. Suddenly, Ray's eyes lit up. "They were on time!" he answered.

---

transcontinental *adj.,* crossing the continent
commerce *n.,* business

Talk About It
Tell your teacher or a classmate about the strategies you used to read "Golden Chances." Explain how they helped you get the most out of the story.

Strategy Toolbox

Plan and Monitor Preview the text and set a purpose for reading. Make sure you understand what you read.

Determine Importance Pause to sum up the main ideas in your own words. After you read ask yourself: "What do I want to want to take away from this?"

Ask Questions Ask yourself what the text reminds you of and write down questions. Get inside the writer's head.

Visualize Make mental pictures of the descriptions. Use all your senses to imagine people, places, and events.

Make Connections Link the text to your life, the world, and other texts.

Make Inferences Deepen your understanding by combining what the writer tells you with what you already know.

Synthesize Put new information together with old information to come up with big ideas.

Name ______________________ Date ____________

Nonfiction: What's Your Strategy?

Use strategies while you read "How to Hire the Best."

DID YOU KNOW?

- Most people prepare for interviews by practicing sample questions and answers.
- You can find tips for interviewing online.

Before you read, choose a strategy from the *Strategy Toolbox* on page 176.

1. The type of text I will read:

____

____

____

____

As you read, make sure the strategy you chose works for you.

2. How I make the strategy work:

____

____

____

____

____

____

____

3. Another strategy I used:

____

____

____

____

____

____

____

How to Hire the Best

Do you have what it takes to succeed in an interview? Study the following case to see how you measure up.

What skills does this job require?

The Interview Begins

Ben Lee was the Sandwich Palace manager who always followed the rules in the Sandwich Palace Manager's Handbook. He needed help at his shop, so he put up a "Help Wanted" sign.

Bestha Whurkers, an energetic teenager from Wilson High, was the first applicant. Ben had never interviewed anyone before, so he checked the handbook. *Rule #1: In an interview, find out about the person's hopes and dreams.*

Bestha answered his first question in a clear voice. She declared that her dream job was to become a Chocolate Milkshake Taste Tester. "Somebody has to step up to the challenge," Bestha said confidently.

Bestha Impresses Ben

Ben thought she sounded perfect for the job, but he wanted to be sure. What did the handbook say? *Rule #2: Each employee must have more than one responsibility.* "That is easy," Bestha said, "I can **multitask**. See, I've been **texting** my friends throughout this interview."

Ben moved on to Rule #3. *Ask the applicant about special skills or abilities that would help her or him to*

continued on next page

---

multitask *v.*, do more than one job or task at the same time

texting *v.*, sending electronic messages

4. Another strategy I used:

____

____

____

____

____

____

____

____

How to Hire the Best, continued

succeed at Sandwich Palace. Bestha pointed proudly to what she had written on her job application: "I can distinguish vanilla from chocolate with my eyes closed; I won the Cookie-Crumb Eating Trophy—77th Street Fair (twice)." Bestha seemed amazing.

Ben Makes a Decision

Ben checked the handbook again. *Rule #4: Before you offer the job, explain the benefits.* The manager proudly told Bestha that Sandwich Palace offered free drinks to employees on duty. That suited Bestha.

Ben Lee hired Bestha Whurkers. With the Manager's Handbook and Bestha, Ben was sure that he was on his way to being more successful than ever.

Your Evaluation

How did Ben and Bestha do? Are you prepared to do better?

Talk About It

Tell your teacher or a classmate about the strategies you used to read "How to Hire the Best." Explain how they helped you open up the meaning of the text.

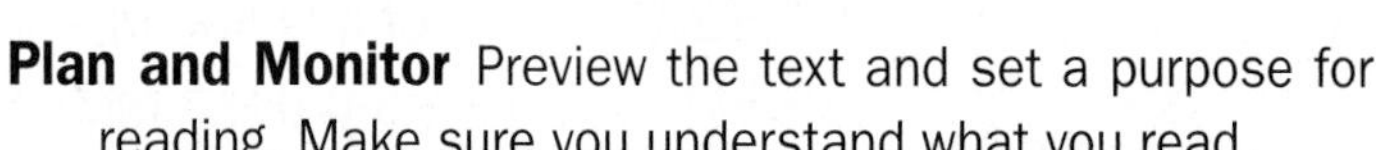

Strategy Toolbox

Plan and Monitor Preview the text and set a purpose for reading. Make sure you understand what you read.

Determine Importance Pause to sum up the main ideas in your own words. After you read ask yourself: "What do I want to want to take away from this?"

Ask Questions Ask yourself what the text reminds you of and write down questions. Get inside the writer's head.

Visualize Make mental pictures of the descriptions. Use all your senses to imagine people, places, and events.

Make Connections Link the text to your life, the world, and other texts.

Make Inferences Deepen your understanding by combining what the writer tells you with what you already know.

Synthesize Put new information together with old information to come up with big ideas.

Name ______________________ Date __________

Categorize

Preview "When Plants Attack" so that you know what to expect when you read. As you read, categorize the information the writer presents.

DID YOU KNOW?

- Photosynthesis is a process by which plants turn the sun's energy into food.
- All food humans eat was a plant at one time.

When Plants Attack

A plant that kills and eats rats. A beautiful flower that smells like rotting meat. Leaves that snap shut and trap startled prey. It isn't science fiction. These plants live right here on Earth.

Carnivorous Plants

Some plants are **carnivorous.** The tropical pitcher feasts on nitrogen from rats and insects that drown in its deep honey pot. The Venus Flytrap also digests meat. When a fly or spider lands on its leaves, the insect's weight triggers a reaction. In one-tenth of a second, the leaves snap shut and the plant consumes the meat.

continued on next page

A tropical pitcher plant

---

carnivorous *adj.*, meat-eating

Categorize the information from this part of the passage in the Idea Diagram.

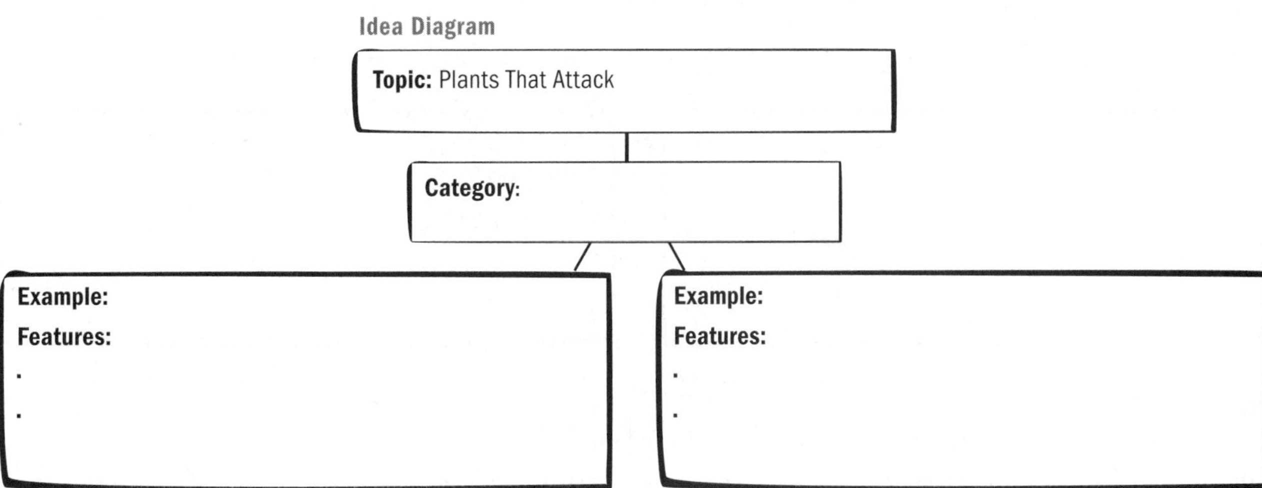

Continue to categorize information as you read the rest of the passage.

When Plants Attack, continued

Parasitic Plants

Parasitic plants are like sneaky thieves. They **latch onto** a host plant to get their nutrients and water. One parasite is the Rafflesia, which starts out as a bud attached to the stem or root of another plant. Taking all its nutrients from its host, the flower grows to three feet wide. This huge flower **emits** the odor of rotting meat. Attracted by the stink, flies land on the plant. Then, the flies carry Rafflesia seeds to other plants. The growth cycle begins again.

The dodder vine is another parasite. Scientists were amazed to discover that this vine identifies a victim through its scent. The vine will twist around a tomato plant and inject needles into the stem and leaves. As the vine sucks out water and nutrients, it chokes the host and nearby plants.

Rafflesia is the world's largest flower.

---

latch onto *v.,* attach themselves
emits *v.,* gives off

Now categorize the information from this part of the passage in the Idea Diagram.

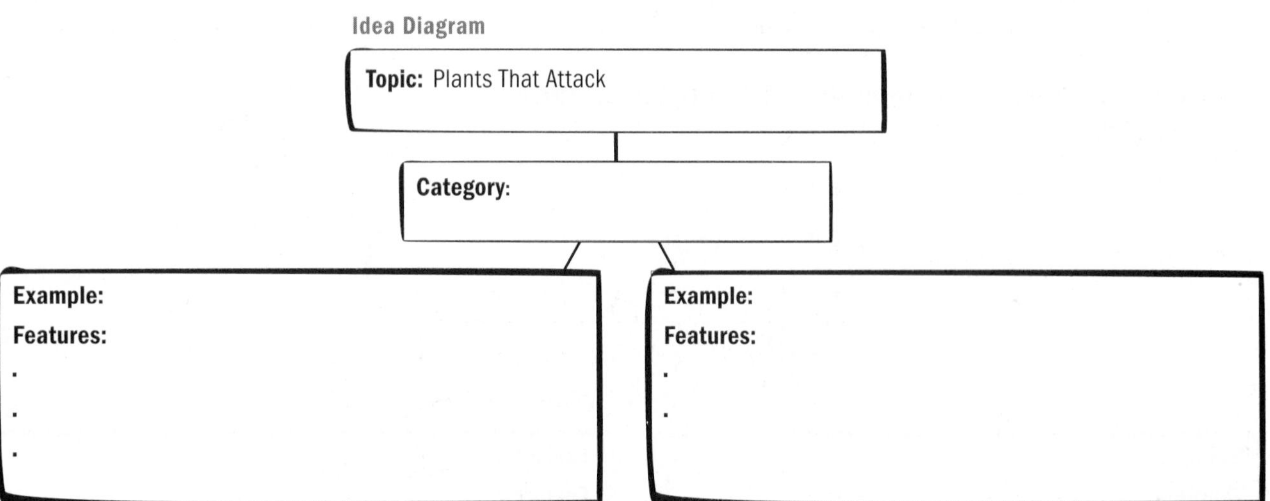

Talk About It

Compare with a classmate how you categorized ideas from the selection. Discuss similarities and differences.

Name ______________________ Date __________

Relate Cause and Effect

Preview "Champion Brothers" so that you know what to expect when you read. As you read, think about the events that cause other events to happen.

DID YOU KNOW?

- Slalom skiers race between poles or gates.
- Giant slalom races are longer and steeper.

Champion Brothers

Peter and Michael Ankeny are only 18 months apart in age. As children they challenged each other in everything—from swimming and tennis to trampoline jumping. This natural competition often led to intense **sibling rivalry**. At the ages of 9 and 7, Peter and Michael took up alpine skiing. Two years later, they began competing in local skiing events. By the age of 10, Michael was winning state and national slalom races. Although he was older, Peter wasn't faring as well. He was often frustrated by his younger brother's success.

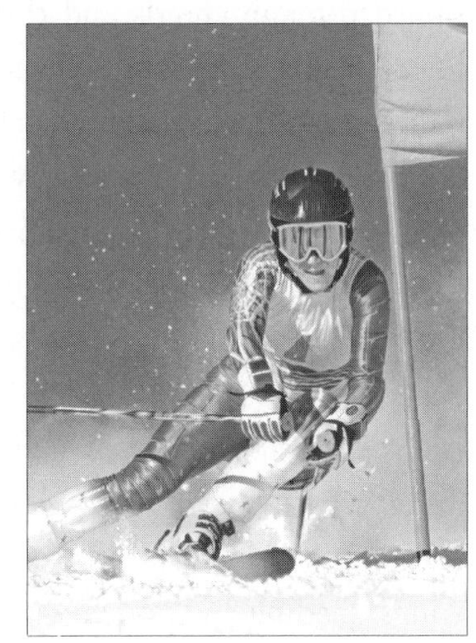

A slalom racer

The rivalry continued into high school. Michael was still winning most of the slalom events. Peter was discouraged but not defeated. His father encouraged him to work harder and take advantage of having Michael as a skiing partner. So, Peter began training with his brother. Peter was pushed to improve his style and technique. As a result, he became a better skier, even reaching the Junior Olympics four times. Today, the brothers are two of Minnesota's best high school alpine skiers. They are still fierce competitors, but now they are **devoted** friends, too.

---

sibling rivalry *n.*, competition between brothers or sisters
devoted *adj.*, dedicated

Use a graphic organizer to show the causes and effects.

Chain of Events

Preview "Alonso's Art" so that you know what to expect when you read. As you read, think about the event that causes other events to happen.

Alonso's Art

Watching from backstage, Alonso was amazed at his brother Jake's performance. Jake's guitar-playing was inspirational. His fingers ripped through chords and then delicately picked out a simple melodic line. The plan was that Alonso would join Jake in a duet. Alonso played well enough to **accompany** his brother, but his heart wasn't in it the way Jake's was. What Alonso really wanted to do was to **sketch** the audience members who were **absorbed** in the music.

Alonso put down his sketch pad when it was time for the duet. *Maybe I'll have time to finish my sketch after the duet,* he thought. During the duet, Alonso missed first one note and then another. *Why keep torturing myself?* Alonso mused. *Jake's talent is making music, but I don't care enough to practice. It's time I stopped trying to be like Jake.*

Alonso went to Jake's next concert without his guitar. He sat in the wings, shading and sketching. He had found his own true talent.

---

accompany *v.,* to play in support of another player
sketch *v.,* to draw quickly
absorbed *adj.,* very interested

Use a graphic organizer to show the cause and multiple effects.

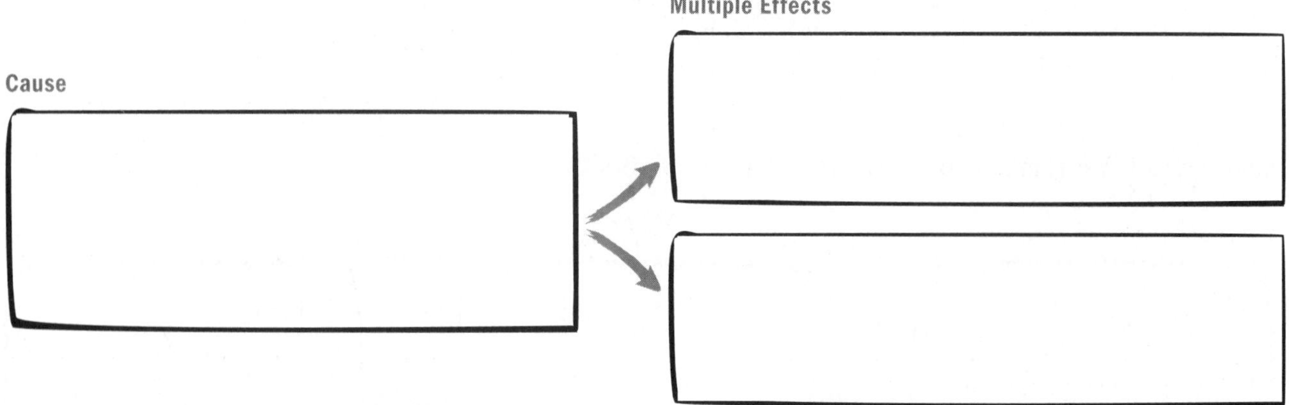

Talk About It

Compare your graphic organizers with a classmate's. Discuss similarities and differences.

Name ______________________ Date ____________

Understand Characters

Preview "Tonya on the Mound" so that you know what to expect when you read. As you read, underline clues to what the main character is like.

DID YOU KNOW?

- In a softball game, a relief pitcher takes the place of the regular pitcher.

TONYA ON THE MOUND

Shoes stay clean when you sit on the bench, and Tonya's **cleats** were spotless. As the only freshman on the team, she knew it was an honor to serve as relief pitcher. Rita, the first-string catcher agreed with Coach's choice. One day, after practice, Tonya overheard Rita talking to Coach.

"That kid Tonya is a good choice. She really knows her stuff."

Tonya's only problem was that Rita never missed a game. How could Tonya prove herself if she never got the chance? Knowing her chance could come at a moment's notice, she analyzed every opposing batter. *Number 23 can't hit curve balls to the outside. Number 12 likes fastballs.*

Then, near the end of the season, Coach signaled Tonya onto the field. It was her time at last! Number 23 stepped to the plate, and she nodded at the catcher. *Curve ball to the outside.* Calmly, Tonya **wound up** and pitched.

---

cleats *n.,* spikes on the bottom of a baseball shoe
wound up *v.,* got ready to throw

Use the graphic organizer to help you understand the character Tonya.

Character: Tonya

This information . . .	Tells me that . . .
Tonya's thoughts:	
Tonya's actions:	
What other characters say about Tonya:	
What the author says about Tonya:	

Preview "When Plans Change" so that you know what to expect when you read. As you read the scene from the play, underline information about the main character Magda.

When Plans Change

ACT TWO

Scene One

MAGDA: (*gazing in disbelief at a letter in her hand*) It was such a long shot. I never thought I would be accepted.

JOSÉ: (*angrily, with an injured expression*) Then why did you apply? You're so impulsive! Did you forget about our plans to work together, like we have the past three summers?

MAGDA: I know . . . But with a college degree from Rogers, who knows what great job I could get?

JOSÉ: (*loudly*) Degree? I thought this was a summer internship! You mean you plan to stay for the full 4-year course?

MAGDA: (*touching Joe's arm gently*) Don't you see? This can be an opportunity for you, too. I haven't forgotten our plans and we can get ideas for our business when you visit me in Boston.

JOSÉ: (*in resignation*) I guess it might work out.

Use the graphic organizer to help you understand the character Magda.

Character: Magda

This information...	Tells me that...
Magda's words:	
Magda's actions:	

Talk About It

Compare your ideas about Tonya and Magda with a classmate's.

Name ______________________ Date ____________

Compare Texts on the Same Topic

Preview "Tech at Street-Level" and "Close That Gap!" so that you know what to expect when you read. As you read each essay, think about the author's viewpoint and purpose.

DID YOU KNOW?

- Students use technology to keep up at school.
- Technology is not available to some students.
- This problem is known as the Digital Divide.

READERS SPEAK

Tech at Street-Level

By Serena Costas, teacher

In this century, almost everyone depends on computers for fun, work, and education. Students who don't have computers at home might face a roadblock to learning. A group of artists and teens are working to remove that impediment. They started Street-Level Youth Media in Chicago's West Town. Street-Level operates three computer centers. They charge no fees.

At Street-Level students learn video production and editing. They do computer animation and web design. Professional artists and technology instructors help them with their projects. For these students, a free computer center is a bridge to future success.

Student using video camera for school project

READERS SPEAK

Close That Gap!

By Anna Silva, student

Like many students at York Community College, I worked diligently to get the opportunity to take classes here. We want to succeed, but we arrive in class lacking computer skills that other students have. It's not our fault. Maybe our elementary and high schools had few computers or old ones. Some of us came to this country recently and did not use computers before. We don't have computers at home.

We're not atypical. Statistics say that only 46% of low-income students use the Internet, but 88% of students from high-income families use it. There's a big gap between students who are used to using technology and those who aren't. York Community College should donate free computers to students like me. It is the only way we can succeed.

Use this chart to compare the authors' purposes and viewpoints.

	Author's Purpose	Author's Viewpoint	Facts and Information
"Tech at Street-Level"			
"Close That Gap!"			

Talk About It

Compare your chart with a classmate's.

Name ______________________ Date ____________

Compare Fiction and Nonfiction

Preview "Over Easy" and "Homeless Myths" so that you know what to expect when you read. As you read the story and the article, think about how they are alike and different.

DID YOU KNOW?

- Homelessness is a big problem in many U.S. cities.
- Many people stereotype homeless persons as beggars.

Over Easy

"Two eggs over easy," Clare shouted over the counter. She hated her job as a waitress. If only there was somebody she could talk to. Then she spotted the new girl, Alicia, outside. She was handing a **disheveled** woman a bag.

When Alicia returned, Clare drew her aside. "What are you doing with that woman?" Clare asked.

"I talked Mr. Melwani into letting her sweep the sidewalk for a meal. I've called a social worker," Alicia said. "She's homeless and just needs a little help."

Clare shrugged and turned away, but she couldn't stop thinking about what Alicia had said. *That woman did remind me of my grandmother*, she thought.

"Want to read this article about homeless people?" Alicia asked as she passed Clare at closing time.

Clare nodded slowly. "Thanks. I think I will."

---

disheveled *adj.*, messy, untidy

Homeless Myths

What are your beliefs about homeless people? Are your ideas based on fact? Here are the most common **myths** about the homeless and data from studies that **contradict** those myths.

Myth #1: Most homeless people expect handouts from working people. *Fact*: Many homeless people have jobs but cannot find affordable housing.

Myth #2: The homeless don't want to go to shelters. *Fact*: In many communities, there are not enough shelters to house all the homeless.

Myth #3: Most homeless people are homeless by choice. *Fact*: The vast majority of homeless people would far prefer to sleep in their own beds at night. Most are homeless because of a traumatic event such as divorce, a death in the family, or loss of a home or a job.

What do you believe now?

---

myths *n.*, ideas not based on facts
contradict *v.*, prove to be untrue

Complete the chart below to compare the passages.

	"Over Easy"	"Homeless Myths"
Author's Purpose		
Organization		
Information		
Viewpoint		
Important Ideas		

Now think about both passages. Tell what you have learned about the problem of homelessness.

____

____

____

____

Talk About It

Compare your chart with a classmate's. Discuss how the authors' purposes, organization, information, and viewpoints are similar and how they differ.

Name ____________________ Date __________

Draw Conclusions

Preview "Waves of Disaster" so that you know what to expect when you read. As you read, underline important facts in the article.

DID YOU KNOW?

- A tsunami is an unusually large ocean wave.
- Earthquakes, landslides, and volcanic activity can cause tsunamis.

Waves of Disaster

Destructive waves hit the coast of Somalia on December 26, 2004. Earlier that day, the tsunami began off the coast of Indonesia. TV news had broadcast the disaster worldwide, but that warning failed to help Somalia. The country had been without an **effective** government since 1991. It was not able to warn its coastal cities of the coming tsunami. Hundreds of Somalis died and thousands lost their homes and livelihoods.

Damage from the tsunami of December 26, 2004, Sri Lanka

Volunteers arrived to help the survivors, but they faced obstacles. Roads were damaged and filled with **debris**. Mules helped aid workers carry medical supplies, food, and blankets to the victims.

The relief effort came slowly. Meanwhile, the people struggled to rebuild their lives.

---

effective *adj.*, working the way it should
debris *n.*, trash left by a disaster

Now record the facts on the notes below. Add them up to draw a conclusion.

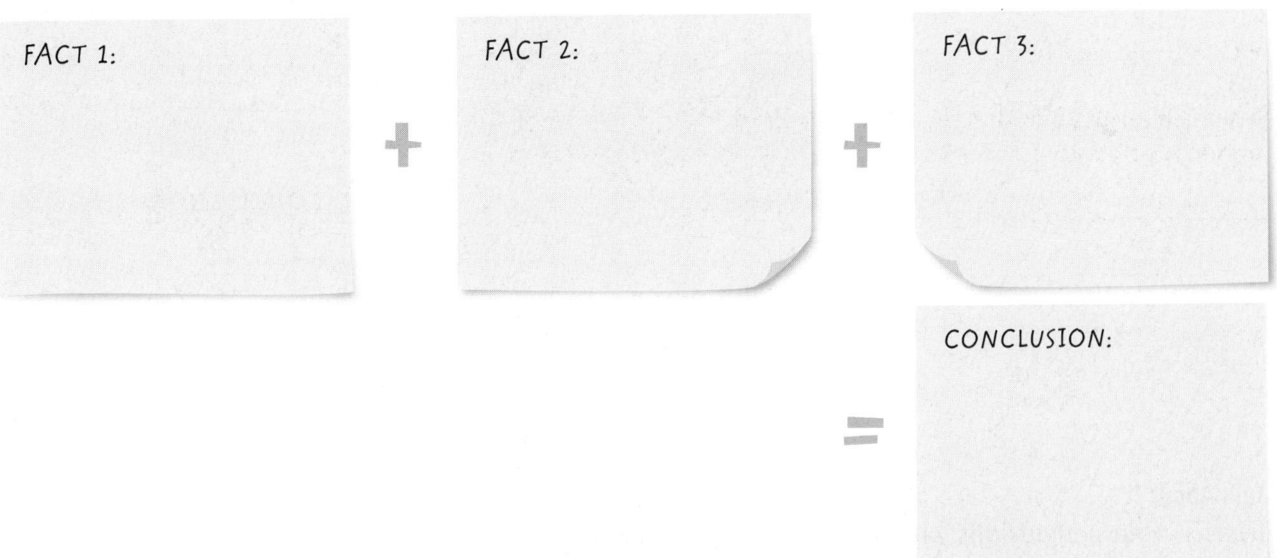

Preview "Lost Treasure" so that you know what to expect when you read. As you read, underline important details.

LOST TREASURE

"Do you have the album *Wild Wanderer?*" Peter asked at the recycled records store.

"I don't think so—classics like that never stay on the shelf for long," the clerk shrugged.

Peter knew his problem was **insurmountable.** The record he had lost was not just collectible, it was autographed. Peter's father had met the band when they appeared at a local concert in 1975, long before Peter was born. The autographed album was a souvenir from what his dad called "the best day of my life."

"Well, will you look?" said Peter **dejectedly.** "I absolutely have to replace it."

"You're in luck," the clerk grinned. "I just happen to have a copy."

---

insurmountable *adj.,* impossible to solve
dejectedly *adv.,* very sadly

Now record the details on the notes below. Add them up to draw a conclusion.

Talk About It

Discuss your conclusions with a classmate. Did you reach the same conclusions?

Name ______________________ Date __________

Identify Details in Fiction

Preview "The Mystery in the Woods" so that you know what to expect when you read. As you read, underline details about the setting. Circle details about the characters.

The Mystery in the Woods

"Eric, wait!" Josh scrambled over a rock outcropping while Eric strode ahead, squinting in the twilight. He suddenly stopped and pointed. A red sports car sat almost hidden by tall grasses and cottonwood saplings. Eric motioned to his friend to come closer, but Josh held back. He was worried the car had something to do with Mr. Beasly's mysterious disappearance. It seemed **reckless** to snoop around.

"Stop worrying," Eric said. "Let's find out why the car is here." He took off his neck bandana, placed it over the car door handle, and opened the door.

The car was empty inside and smelled of **mildew**, like a damp basement. Eric jumped into the front seat. Josh slid into the passenger seat, opened the glove box, and found the registration. "This is Ms. Santos's car. I remember when it was stolen last year."

Eric snapped photographs with his cell phone. "Wait until everyone sees this!"

---

reckless *adj.*, dangerous, risky
mildew *n.*, a fungus that grows in damp environments

How do the details about setting help create a mood?

____

____

____

How do the details about the characters show what they are like?

____

____

____

Preview "The Missing Clue" so that you know what to expect when you read. As you read, underline details about the plot of the story.

THE MISSING CLUE

Officer Lara Hill had investigated dozens of burglaries in her time. But this one was different. The victim was **reluctant** to press charges. Witnesses were almost **nonexistent**. Nothing seemed to add up.

"This means we just have to go back to basic police work," Hill said to her partner, Ray Ngu.

The officers returned to the crime scene for another look. As before, the apartment looked trashed and a breeze blew through the open window. So, what were they missing?

"Wait a minute," Ngu yelled from the kitchen. "Looks like a phone number on this." He held out a crumpled note he'd found in a kitchen drawer.

When Ngu punched in the number, a phone rang in the apartment next door.

"Well, what do you know," Hill said. "Sounds like the neighbor knows the victim more than he said."

After calling for a search warrant, the officers used a master key to enter the apartment next door. There on the coffee table, in plain sight, lay all the items missing from the victim's apartment.

"If we can locate the neighbor, we've got ourselves an arrest," Hill commented.

---

reluctant *adj.*, not willing
nonexistent *adj.*, do not exist

How do the details about the plot build suspense?

____

____

____

____

Talk About It

Tell a classmate about the methods the writer uses to build suspense.

Name ______________________ Date ____________

Distinguish Fact and Opinion

Preview the two passages so that you know what to expect when you read. As you read, underline the facts and circle the opinions in the passages.

ElectraCize is the only Teen Fitness Center in the tri-state region.

At ElectraCize you can do it all. Play video games while you work up a sweat. ElectraCize packs in the most fun of any gym in town!

Sign up today!

EDITORIAL

Exercise to Lose Stress

We know exercise is a great way to get a perfect physique. It does more than tone muscles and burn fat, though. Exercise can also help students deal with many problems.

Doctors recommend exercising at least 45 minutes per day. Many teens exercise less than 45 minutes per week! Our school should allow stressed students to do short workouts during the day. Many students feel apprehensive about exams. They also have anxiety from personal conflicts. Exercise is the best way to deal with the stress from these problems.

Read each statement and tell if it is a fact or opinion. Explain how you can tell.

Statement	Fact or Opinion?	How Can You Tell?
ElectraCize Your Life! "ElectraCize is the only Teen Fitness Center in the tri-state region."		
ElectraCize Your Life! "ElectraCize packs in the most fun of any gym in town!"		
Exercise to Lose Stress "Our school should allow stressed students to do short workouts during the day."		
Exercise to Lose Stress "Exercise is the best way to deal with the stress from these problems."		

Preview "How Fit Are We?" so that you know what to expect when you read. As you read, underline the facts and circle the opinions.

How Fit Are We?

Many experts consider **obesity** and lack of fitness an epidemic in the U.S. The average young child today is fatter than the average child was 50 years ago. One cause is that people are eating too much. Even more important is the fact that people don't get enough exercise on a regular basis.

Studies show that nearly half of youths from ages 12–21 in America today do not exercise every day. In the future, the number may drop even more. Schools are not emphasizing physical education as much as in the past. This is especially true for students in higher grades. Fewer than six percent of all high schools provide daily physical education.

Moderate daily physical activity can have **beneficial** effects on the human body. Exercising builds strong bones and muscles. Physical activity also helps to keep blood pressure at a healthy level.

Running is one way to get daily exercise.

---

obesity *n.,* condition of extreme overweight
beneficial *adj.,* positive

Read each statement and tell if it is a fact or opinion. Explain how you can tell.

Statement	Fact or Opinion?	Why?
How Fit Are We? "Many experts consider obesity and lack of fitness an epidemic in the U.S."		
How Fit Are We? "Fewer than six percent of all high schools provide daily physical education."		
How Fit Are We? "Physical activity also helps to keep blood pressure at a healthy level."		

Talk About It

Talk with a classmate about other things you've read about fitness and the writers' facts and opinions.

Name ______________________ Date ____________

Make Inferences

Preview "Climate Changes in the Arctic" so that you know what to expect when you read. As you read, make inferences about what may happen to the Inuit people.

DID YOU KNOW?

- The Inuit are native people in Arctic regions.
- They share common culture and language.

Climate Changes in the Arctic

The Inuit have lived in coastal areas in the Arctic Circle for more than one thousand years. But the future is uncertain for the **indigenous** peoples and their traditions.

The Inuit **rely** on hunting. Recently, sea ice has thinned because of warmer sea temperatures. Caribou, and the hunters tracking them, have fallen through the ice.

House foundations weaken as the ground thaws. This causes the structures to lean. Coastal communities may be wiped out if melting ice causes sea levels to rise.

Inuit woman fishing Baffin Island, Nunavut, Canada

indigenous *adj.*, native
rely *v.*, depend

Combine what the writer says with what you know to make an inference.

What the Writer Says	+	What I Know	=	Inference

Preview "The Mysterious Tutor" so that you know what to expect when you read. As you read the story, make inferences about the characters.

The Mysterious Tutor

Ty groaned as he shut his algebra book.

"Tough test?" the man on the bench next to Ty asked.

"Yeah, next Friday," Ty replied **dismally.**

"I'm Cal. Maybe I can help."

Ty glanced again at the man's dirty clothes and tangled hair. He held a **tattered** copy of *Pro Chef.* "Well, maybe..." *Anything was worth a try,* Ty thought.

Ty and Cal met at the community center every day for the next week to study algebra. To Ty's surprise, Cal seemed to have answers to every one of Ty's questions. The odd thing was that every example Cal used to illustrate a mathematical concept had to do with cooking. Although Ty was curious about Cal's story, he was too busy studying to ask about it.

---

dismally *adv.,* unhappily
tattered *adj.,* frayed or torn to shreds

Combine details from the story with what you know to make an inference.

Talk About It

Compare your inference to a classmate's. Are your inferences based on the same details? Are your guesses logical?

Name ____________________ Date __________

Identify Main Idea and Details

Preview "A Voice for the Poor" so that you know what to expect when you read. As you read, identify the main idea and the details that support it.

A Voice for the Poor

In the late 1800s, poor people lived in slums, hoping for factory jobs. They had limited access to legal aid, childcare, medical care, and other social services. Yet the need was great. Many people **disregarded** the problems of the poor.

Jane Addams was different. She devoted her life to helping people whom society had forgotten. In 1889, she established Hull House, a social services center for underprivileged families in Chicago. Within two years, Hull House was serving two thousand people each week.

Jane Addams

disregarded *v.,* ignored

Now complete the diagram to show the main idea and the supporting details.

Main Idea

Details

Preview "Fighting for Opportunity" so that you know what to expect when you read. As you read, identify the main idea and details that support it. Trap your thinking in the diagram below.

DID YOU KNOW?

- Apartheid was a policy in South Africa that kept the races separate.

Fighting for Opportunity

Today, some people say that tennis champion Arthur Ashe never considered losing. They see Ashe as the first black person to win the U.S. Open and to be selected to play on the U.S. Davis Cup team. It is equally important, however, to remember his **social activism**.

Ashe expected to compete in a prestigious tennis competition in South Africa. But because of his skin color, the country denied him a **visa**. So Ashe spoke out. After several refusals, he was granted a visa. Ashe became the first black to win a South African Open title. He also drew worldwide attention to the unfair apartheid system. For Ashe, both were important victories.

When asked about the courage his actions displayed, Ashe said, "You've got to get to the stage in life where going for it is more important than winning or losing."

Arthur Ashe, Jr.

---

social activism *n.*, actions to improve society
visa *n.*, official document to enter a country

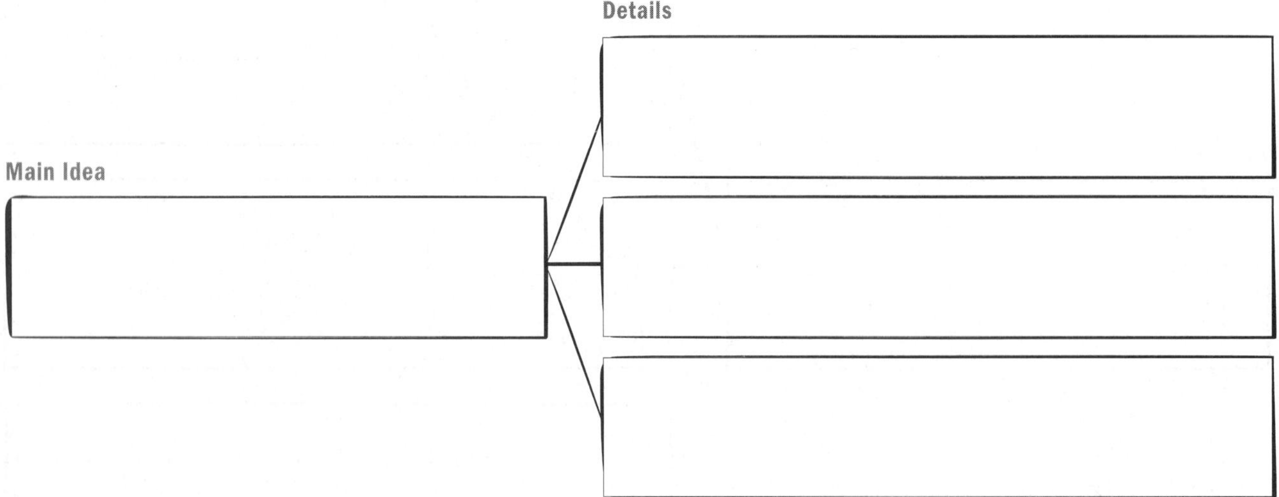

Talk About It

Compare your diagrams with a classmate's. Did you sum up the main ideas in the same why?

Name ______________________ Date ____________

Understand Plot

Preview "Second Chance" so that you know what to expect when you read. As you read the story, use the diagram below to track the plot.

SECOND CHANCE

"Tell me, have you previously been employed?" the manager of the Country Market inquired.

Hands shoved in the back pockets of torn jeans, Ricky's eyes dropped to his shoes and he shook his head.

"And what grade are you in?" Ms. Holland scrutinized the application. Ricky's cell phone rang out interrupting the interview.

"Uh . . . tenth," Ricky mumbled distractedly, answering the phone. When he looked up again, Ms. Holland was gone.

"Back already?" his older sister asked, surprised, when Ricky arrived home. Frowning, she continued, "Bro, did you say you desperately need a job? Because you won't get one looking like that."

Ricky realized she had a point. "OK, I need some tips. Got some?"

His sister was quick to respond. "First, you have to be prepared. Show them that you're serious and responsible. You also have to dress the part. And don't forget to turn off your cell phone!"

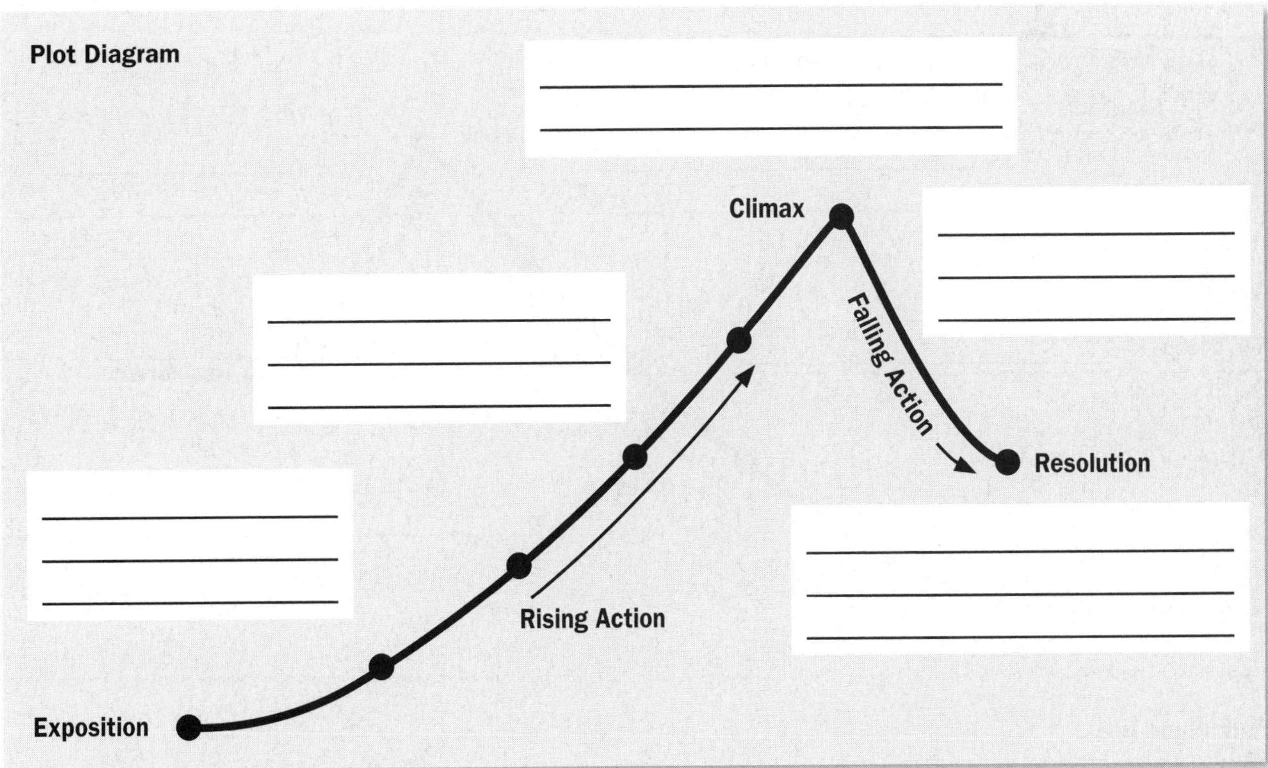

Preview "Election Day Jitters" so that you know what to expect when you read. As you read the scene, use the diagram to track the events in the play.

Election Day Jitters

ACT ONE

Scene One

MARGI *and* **COLIN** *are about to deliver speeches for student council.*

COLIN: (*voice trembling*) I'm really nervous.

MARGI: You'll do fine, Colin. We might not have the most friends, but our idea for a class trip for each grade is brilliant. (*gives Colin a hug*)

Scene Two

MARGI *and* **COLIN** *are on stage in front of the entire student body.*

COLIN: (*at the microphone*) Let's be honest. I'm scared to death. (*grips the lectern*) But I'm not scared to ask you to vote for us.

MARGI: Elect us, and annual class trips will become a reality.

BOTH: (*enthusiastically*) Vote for Myers and McCormick!

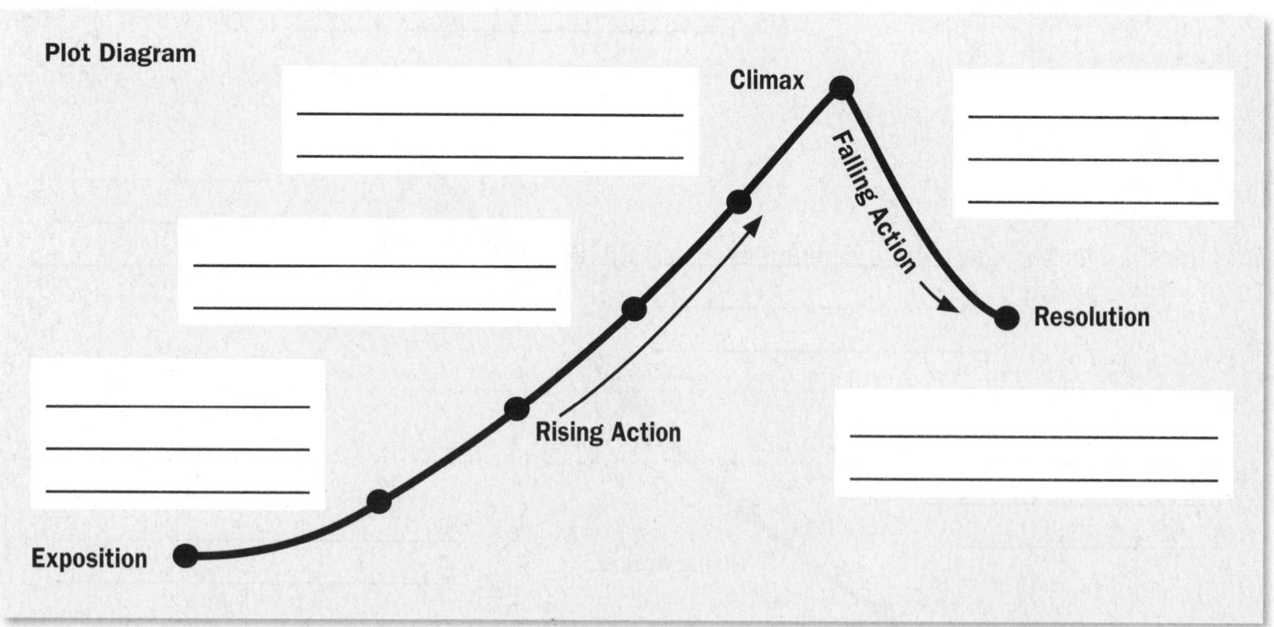

Talk About It

Tell your teacher how tracking the plots helped you follow the action of the story and the play.

Name ______________________ Date ____________

Understand Sequence

Preview the text so that you know what to expect when you read. As you read, pay attention to the order in which events happened.

DID YOU KNOW?

- Dolores Huerta used nonviolent tactics to improve the lives of migrant workers.
- César Chávez was a Mexican-American farm worker, civil rights activist, and labor leader.

Dolores Huerta, Teacher and Organizer

What power do powerless people have? Dolores Huerta believed they have the power to organize. As a young teacher in California, Huerta taught the children of **migrant** farm workers. Huerta saw many students coming to school hungry. So she quit teaching and decided to help her students' parents gain power.

In 1962, Huerta co-founded the United Farm Workers (UFW) with civil rights leader César Chávez. The struggle to gain power was never easy. The workers suffered through strikes, protests, and even violent attacks. In 1966, the UFW was able to **negotiate** better labor contracts. Later, the farm workers won the first medical, retirement, and safety plans in the history of agriculture. During these years of struggle, Huerta gained respect as a leader and a fearless activist. She was one of the most outspoken spokespersons of her time. She was even key in helping Robert F. Kennedy's presidential campaign of 1968.

Dolores Huerta rallies farm workers, August 22, 2002

migrant *adj.*, moving from place to place
negotiate *v.*, argue for

Use the time line to show the sequence of important events in Dolers Huerta's life.

Time Line of Huerta's Life

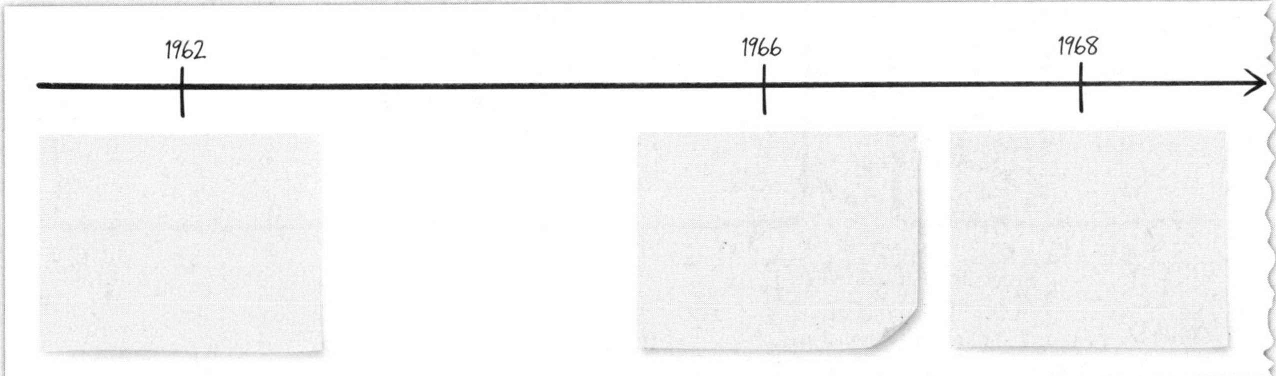

Preview "Things Change" so that you know what to expect when you read. As you read the story, pay attention to the sequence of events.

DID YOU KNOW?

- Every year about 40,000 people in the U.S. move.

THINGS CHANGE

When Dan was 19, he decided to return to Bentonville. Everything about the place looked unfamiliar as the bus **trundled** past Memorial Park. Dan remembered **rifling** through CDs at the Music Stop three years before and slurping milkshakes at the Dairy Dream. Now, a bustling supermarket had replaced the record store, and if he wanted ice cream, he would have to drive to a sprawling mall.

Dan was returning to Bentonville partly to visit his aunt. But his mind was on his childhood friend, Charlie. Dan's family moved from Ohio to Tucson when he was sixteen. At first, he and Charlie had emailed every day. But last year the emails had **dwindled**.

Dan stared outside. The town had changed. Had Charlie?

A few hours later Dan walked to Charlie's house. When the door opened, a grinning young woman stood before him. "Dan!"

---

trundled *v.*, rolled
rifling *v.*, flipping
dwindled *v.*, became fewer and fewer

Use a sequence chain to record the sequence of events in the story. Use an arrow to show a flashback.

Sequence Chain

Talk About It

Compare your time line and sequence chain with a classmate's.

Name ______________________ Date ____________

Identify Setting

Preview the story so that you know what to expect when you read. As you read, underline words that describe the setting. Think about how the setting affects the characters and the mood.

DID YOU KNOW?

- Ancient Greece depended heavily on trade by sea.
- On open water, high winds often cause bad storms.

An Ancient Voyage

Adara looked at the horizon. "The winds **portend** stormy weather soon," she said. "We must be underway within the hour."

Her brothers, Lander and Panos, loaded the ship with goods to trade just as they had since childhood. In Athens, the three would trade their wools for supplies needed at home.

The Mediterranean Sea was the only way to transport the wools to market. Yet the risks were **daunting**. As the ship set out, the sails filled with angry gusts of wind. At first Adara hoped to outrun the storm, but soon it was clear they would have to take shelter along the coast.

continued on next page

---

portend *v.*, give clues to
daunting *v.*, very challenging

Use the chart to record the details about the setting and the characters' reactions. In the last column, describe the mood these details create.

Details About the Setting	Characters' Reactions	Mood

Continue reading the story and underlining words that describe the setting.

An Ancient Voyage, continued

Adara looked for the coast, but the churning sea seemed to have swallowed it. Her brothers expertly swung the sails around, and the boat **pivoted.** Lightning flashed beneath the rumbling thunder. The dark sky swirled and rain pelted the ship.

Adara feared the winds would break their wooden ship into splinters on the rocky shoreline. Through the driving rain, Lander gestured toward a cove a bit further along the coast.

"Bring the boat to shore!" yelled Panos.

Adara fought the rudder in the powerful waves. A roaring gust lashed the vessel and the boat threatened to **capsize.** Adara struggled to hold her course.

Finally, the ship entered the cove and Adara smiled. In spite of the danger, the sea held the key to their fortune.

---

pivoted *v.,* turned sharply
capsize *v.,* flip over

Use the chart to record the details about the setting and the characters' reactions. In the last column, describe the mood these details create.

Details About the Setting	Characters' Reactions	Mood
	Adara: Lander: Panos:	

Talk About It

Talk to a classmate about how the setting affects the characters and plot of the story.